UNDER PRESSURE

HOW THE GOSPEL HELPS US HANDLE THE PRESSURES OF WORK

Andrew Laird

First published in 2017 by City Bible Forum

National Library of Australia Cataloguing-in-Publication entry:

Creator:	Laird, Andrew, author.
Title:	Under pressure: how the gospel helps us handle the pressures of work
ISBN:	978-0-6481379-6-2 (paperback)

Printed by Lightning Source
Text design by Green Hill Publishing
Cover image by sorbetto/iStock.com
Cover design by Gina Walters
Editorial services by Gina Denholm

CONTENTS

INTRODUCTION: UNDER PRESSURE

My eyes glazed over. It felt like just yesterday that I had heard this same presentation, been shown this same infographic and signed this same form acknowledging that 'I, Andrew Laird, have completed the annual company Occupational Health and Safety training'.

Most workplaces have them - the annual (or perhaps more frequent) training session outlining how to stay safe while on the job. And while I jest about mind-numbing OH&S presentations, workplace safety is, of course, no laughing matter. Some workplaces - construction sites, factory floors, hospitals - are filled with potential dangers.

But workplace injuries are not confined to the so-called blue-collar jobs. There is a rising form of workplace injury that occurs in the office - an injury that does not affect the arms, the legs or even the back. According to one work safety organisation, the part of the body most likely to be injured in the office is the 'psychological system'. Currently, 27% of all office injuries are caused by 'work-related stress from work pressure'.[1]

Whatever kind of work you do – in an office or not – you probably need little convincing of the pressures of work. According to one report, three out of every five Australian workers report having a mental health issue as a result of their work. On average, three days of the leave a worker takes each year are due to workplace stress.[2]

And as Christians, rightly or wrongly, we sometimes feel this pressure even more than our colleagues. In addition to all the pressures of work life, family life and social life that we share with our colleagues, we have the added responsibilities that come with being part of a church community: regular Sunday services, morning tea rosters, evenings out with Bible study, church weekends away – the list goes on.

We are under pressure.

What is pressure?

Recently I had lunch with a friend. Over the course of our hour together he spoke about his work, using the word 'pressure' at least seven times! It was clearly the defining word of his current experience.

In fact, it's rare for me to catch up with someone these days without hearing them use the word pressure at some point in our conversation.[3] Whether it's time pressure, financial pressure, social pressure, pressure at home or pressure at work, pressure seems to be *the* word for many of us in describing how we feel.

But what is it?

---

1. worksafe.vic.gov.au/hotspots#/office (accessed 19 July 2017).
2. afuturethatworks.org.au/reports (accessed 19 July 2017).
3. Of course, I've become highly attuned to noticing the word while I've been working on this book!

The Oxford dictionary defines pressure as 'continuous physical force exerted on or against an object by something in contact with it', or 'the use of persuasion or intimidation to make someone do something'.[4] It is the idea of being squeezed, pushed, or pressed in by something or someone. When it comes to work, it might be a boss, colleague or client who is pressing in on you with demands, expectations and responsibilities.

However, as we'll discover, there is a lot more to pressure than this simple definition contains. Pressure isn't always caused by something outside of us. It isn't always a negative thing. Perhaps the best news of all is that the Christian faith understands, brings perspective to and provides solutions for our pressures.

The causes of our pressure

You are feeling squeezed, pushed and pressed in, especially at work. You are under pressure. But why? Here are the five most common reasons I have encountered:

1. The wealth of choices we enjoy

Many of us in the West live in a time and a place where we enjoy great wealth, and with it countless options for what we eat and drink, what we wear, what entertainment we enjoy and, for many, what we do for work. Some of you may feel more limited than this, but before you try and tell me that there are plenty of people better off than you, if you enjoy *any* of the above choices then by world standards you are wealthy.

Now, I think that this level of choice is a great blessing. You won't hear me trying to make you feel guilty for being in such a privileged position. But some of us might have wondered if all this choice is a

---

4. oxforddictionaries.com.

reason for our pressure. We feel a pressure to 'have it all' because there are so many good things to choose from.

2. The changing way we work

Adding to our overwhelm is the way that the working world has radically changed in the last twenty to thirty years. Many of us now do what is described as 'knowledge work', where the main commodity is information rather than physical materials. It's sometimes described as 'thinking for a living'.

Knowledge work doesn't have the same constraints as agricultural or even manufacturing work. There are no limits to how much of it can be done and, with the advances in technology, no limits to where it can be done either. Apart from face-to-face meetings, almost all the other work I do can be performed just about anywhere so long as I have my laptop and access to wi-fi.

All of this has led to changes to office spaces (the rise of hot-desking), expectations from employers (employees are always able to respond to messages), and when we work ('I'll just do a few emails after dinner'). Work is always present, and this causes pressure.

3. The people we work with

Our work involves more than just dealing with information and knowledge. We also have to deal with people: colleagues, clients and customers. Often, these people contribute to the pressure of work just as much as the tasks themselves.

I spend most of my working days talking with other Christians about their work and the pressures that they are facing. Most times, it's not the work itself they talk to me about, but the people they work with. I've often joked with people that leading a staff team would be easy if you didn't have the staff to deal with!

4. The pressure to fit in

For the Christian person in the workplace, there is often an additional pressure. Plenty of workplaces are shaped and governed by a worldview that is profoundly at odds with the Christian view of the world. Some Christians feel daily pressure to modify their values and ethics in order to fulfil the requests of a colleague or a superior. There is a pressure to 'conform to the pattern of this world' (Romans 12:2).

Of course, Christians are not the only people who feel the pressure to adapt their behaviour in order to fit in with those around them. Feeling pressured to conform to a group is a culture-wide experience. However, there is an added level of pressure when values arising from the Christian worldview rub up against workplace values. At times, the pressure to go along with the values that drive organisations, corporations, the market or even just the person at the desk next to me can feel almost inescapable.

5. The need to keep on top of everything

In recent years, sleep has joined exercise and diet as one of the three essential ingredients that experts say we need in order to have a healthy life. Yet when it comes to prioritising sleep, many of us fall far short of what our bodies require. And what's to blame for this? One big contributor to our sleep deficit is the pressure we feel to keep on top of everything, especially our work.

For many of us this deficit comes from staying up late. We slump into bed most nights later than we had hoped because there is just too much to do. Perhaps we stay up watching TV, desperate for that 'down time' we missed after working late yet again. Or there's a late night email from a colleague or client and we think that dealing with it at 11 pm will lighten the load in the morning. For others of us (and this is my problem) it's not the staying up late, but the middle-of-the-night wake-ups where we find our minds racing with worry, fretting over the workload that awaits our attention in the morning.

One way or the other, the pressure to keep on top of everything has a detrimental impact upon our sleep.

How to handle the pressure

There are likely other reasons why you feel under pressure at work – uncertainty about how to solve a particular task, or computer problems first thing on Monday morning. But let us start with these five big ones: 1) How do we handle the pressure to 'have it all'? 2) What about the pressure of ever-present work? 3) How do we handle the pressure of difficult workplace relationships? 4) What about that added pressure for Christians to conform? And finally, 5) What can we do about the pressure to keep on top of everything that impacts our sleep?

For me, these questions are in no way theoretical; they are deeply personal. The quest to handle pressure is one that I have been on since I began full-time, paid employment. While university assessment deadlines were sometimes stressful, it wasn't until my first job as a journalist and radio newsreader that I encountered real pressure for the first time. For eight hours every day, I worked with an hourly deadline. Every hour, whether I was ready or not, the news theme would begin playing and I had to be in the studio in front of the microphone ready with five minutes of news to read, timing out to the exact second. And I had to sound polished and calm, even when I'd sprinted into the studio as the news theme was already playing because I'd been scrambling to finish writing my script. For those years, there was no such thing as a lunchbreak and sometimes not even a toilet break.

While the pressure was incredibly intense for those hours at work, it was also the kind of pressure that I could walk away from at the end of each day. These days, my work pressures come in the form of big projects that require several weeks (or months) of attention. This makes for a different kind of pressure, the kind that hangs over you constantly and increases anxiety levels as deadlines get closer. Added to that is a pressure I have of juggling two work roles and their different responsibilities, working with my wife to look after our growing family, my church commitments, study commitments, kids' school commitments, extended family commitments – and to cap it all off, a bunch of deadlines for a book about pressure.

I know that I'm not alone in feeling this. I know that you could easily change the details in my story above and paint a similarly pressured picture of yourself. I know, because I've spent most of my working days for the last four years talking with people like you about the pressure you're under, and working out together how we can handle it.

What I've discovered is that the Bible has real answers to these modern workplace pressures, in particular those five that I have outlined. As we explore them, you will notice that some of these pressures are *external*, relating to the people around us or the work culture we're a part of – things outside of us squeezing, pushing and pressing in on us to cause pressure. But some of these pressures are *internal*, reflecting something of our hearts. Large amounts of the pressure we experience might, in fact, be self-imposed. A mixture of internal and external pressures is at work in our lives.

So in this book, as we consider the various reasons for our pressure and ways forward, I've included some short action boxes. Some of these contain reflections to help with *habit changes* – practical steps we can take that will help us alleviate some of our pressure. And some of these boxes contain reflections to help with *heart changes* – short questions that will help us get to the core of some of our problems with pressure. These action boxes also reflect the fact that I don't consider this book alone to be *the solution* to your pressure, merely *a contribution* to your quest to handle it better. We each need to work through the details specific to our own situation. There is no 'one size fits all' answer.

But there is one thing that we all need to help us handle pressure. And that is the gospel. I'm convinced that God's good news for us in Jesus addresses our problems with pressure and paves the way to the changed hearts and habits that will help us to handle it. There is hope for those under pressure. Let's discover it.

1

HOW TO HANDLE... THE PRESSURE TO 'HAVE IT ALL'

As I write this, I am sitting in a Melbourne cafe drinking a long black. It was just one of a dozen of drinks on the menu to choose from. Like the options before me at my cafe, there is also no shortage of choice of location I could work on this from. I could have stayed in my office or gone to the local library. But this cafe is good because it is just near the supermarket and I need to pick up some yoghurt for my kids on the way home. Nothing fancy, just vanilla flavoured, though now I think about it I'll have to choose between low fat, no fat or biodynamic organic. Or maybe I should go for the tasty, high-sugar option and have the kids bouncing off the walls. (Actually, maybe that choice is pretty straightforward.)

Choices when it comes to coffee. Choices when it comes to where I work. Choices when it comes to yoghurt. For someone like me who loves efficiency, I find my desire for simplicity increasingly thwarted by overwhelming choice. Even purchasing a simple tub of vanilla yoghurt is not so simple.

You've likely noticed this wealth of choices that we enjoy. If not, take a moment to pause next time you are walking through a supermarket and notice the array of possibilities before you and what it says about our society. We are spoilt for choice. We are the options generation. The alternatives seem limitless.

The choices we face in a single supermarket aisle are merely an illustration for the rest of life. Think about the possibilities that you have available when it comes to choosing a cafe or restaurant. It is the same when it comes to holidays and travel. Searching for a hotel in the Brisbane CBD on a travel website recently, I was given 106 options to choose from. Entertainment is no different: on average, Hollywood releases 600 films each year. On a single weekend in my home city of Melbourne there are usually four or five major sporting fixtures. On my phone there is always another app I just *have* to download. And there is a very real pressure to not miss out on any of this but to try and 'have it all'.

A culture of trying to have it all

The push to have it all is everywhere we go. In all spheres of life – home, work, community, church – there is a pressure not to miss a single opportunity or experience. As one writer starkly observes, 'having it all has become a widespread aspiration in Western society'.[5]

And in some ways it makes perfect sense. When we enjoy the wealth and prosperity that we do in the West and the choices that such wealth provides, of course we want to enjoy, experience and have it all.

---

5. Roman Krznaric, *How to Find Fulfilling Work*, (London: Macmillan, 2012), 114.

'Having it all' at work

When it comes to the workplace, we can find the same dazzling array of choices before us. The options don't end when we finish our vocational training or university degree and land that first job. There are training courses to attend, professional development to undertake and numerous other ways to grow and develop our careers. We may consider enrolling in an MBA, a master's degree or a PhD, or even retraining for a different type of work.

In a knowledge-based industry, there is always the potential for adding another great idea to the to-do list. In my current line of work, there is always another article I could write, paper I could read or presentation I could construct. The list feels endless.

This pressure can look very different for each of us depending on the season of life that we are in, but it is still the same pressure. For some of us it might look like piling full-time study onto full-time work to ensure that we stay one step ahead in our industry and don't miss out on any career opportunities. For others, pressure may look like both spouses working full-time with some extra study thrown in, as well as trying not to miss out on 'seeing the world' on holidays. Even in retirement we can feel the pressure, juggling grandkids, extensive travel, volunteer work and the odd bit of paid consultancy work that might come our way, not wanting to miss out on any of it.

'Having it all' as a family

There is one season of life where the pressure to 'have it all' can take its biggest toll for those of us who are married – the time when we have children living at home. For many people this is a period when dad, mum or both are establishing careers and pursuing more career achievements – another degree, another publication, a certain recognition – and working long hours while also raising the kids. Sometimes it's not the career achievements but the pursuit of a certain lifestyle – size of home, car or holiday – that necessitates a certain level of income, driving dad, mum or both to take on long hours of paid employment.

This pressure only increases when we throw into the mix the choices on offer to children today. Extracurricular activities for kids abound, whether it's learning a musical instrument (but which one?), playing a sport (again, lots to choose from), taking up dancing (which style?) or receiving some extra academic tutoring.

Parents are spoilt for choice. Kids are spoilt for choice. There are so many good things to enjoy and we're all working hard to try and make sure we don't miss out on any of it. For some, this frantic family culture is the *key* cause of their pressure.

Roman Krznaric, in his book *How to Find Fulfilling Work*, shares about how he tries to have it all and the frantic family culture that ensues. He describes a morning argument with his wife about who will stay home to look after their sick three-year old twins that day. 'She's an economist at a development-aid agency, busy writing a report . . . I'm struggling to meet my dead-line to finish a book on how to find fulfilling work'.[6] Roman goes on to provide a number of practical ways to handle the pressure to have it all, including the following piece of advice: 'Having it all doesn't mean you must have it all at the same time . . . [stretch] your ambition to "have it all" over an extended time span.'[7] While he recognises our finitude, he still doesn't give up the dream of having it all.

All seasons of life (single, married, married with kids, retirement) have their own version of what having it all looks like, and each one can leave us suffering from what Tom Smith from the University of Chicago calls OBL: 'overwhelmed by life'.[8] Perhaps in certain moments you've recognised this cultural pressure to have it all, and

---

6. Krznaric, *How to Find Fulfilling Work*, 113.
7. Krznaric, *How to Find Fulfilling Work*, 119.
8. Brigid Schulte, *Overwhelmed: Work, Love and Play When No One Has the Time*, (New York: Piccador, 2015), 26.

maybe even thought that it could be a key cause of all your pressure. Or maybe you have unthinkingly adopted a 'have it all' approach to life no different from your friends, family and colleagues. Either way, you're feeling the pressure that comes from trying to do too much, to try every choice available. And you've wondered what the solution is.

Mindfulness: The solution within?

Given the widespread scale of this pressure, it is little surprise that there's been a rising movement in recent years to try and alleviate some of it. One solution, it is said, is within. That solution is mindfulness.

Mindfulness has come to mean so many different things. At its core it is a meditation technique where you focus on the present moment, notice what you are thinking, feeling and sensing. You accept that moment without judgement so that you may regulate your thoughts, emotions and behaviours. Doing this can help relieve pressure.

With stress the number one cause of office injuries, the practice of mindfulness is taking workplaces by storm. One employee I know recently attended a mindfulness training session as part of Safe Work Month at her office. Other workplaces have opened mindfulness rooms. And one of the technology culprits is now trying to become the saviour. On my iPhone there is a Health app which, along with tracking my sleep, diet and exercise, also allows me to record my daily 'Mindfulness Minutes' – although that kind of defeats the purpose, because now I am feeling pressure to get my mindfulness minutes up for the day!

Mindfulness, however, has come to encompass much more than meditation. In some of those workplace mindfulness rooms you can learn yoga, make a healthy smoothie or enjoy some colouring in.

All of these modes of relaxation can have positive effects. But even the experts recognise that mindfulness can only go so far. Philip Bohle, Professor of Work and Health at Sydney University, says this of mindfulness techniques: 'I am sure they often enhance people's lives and they also can be quite useful for coping with excessive demands at work, as long as those demands are short-lived . . . But I don't think they are an adequate solution to workplaces where workloads are chronically excessive'.[9]

In situations of chronic stress, Professor Bohle says, mindfulness is 'a bandaid'. It's a temporary fix for a bigger problem, one that cannot be solved simply by looking within to what we're thinking, feeling and sensing. What's more, in so many instances, the problem that mindfulness is trying to solve is not actually external, but internal. We place ourselves under pressure by trying to have it all. It's a problem that already lies within us.

The problem within

Jeremiah 17:9 contains perhaps the clearest explanation of why looking within to find the solution is rarely going to solve our problems. 'The heart is deceitful above all things and beyond cure. Who can understand it?' The pressure to have it all stems from heart problems.

A dissatisfied, discontent heart

Oftentimes, the pursuit to have it all reveals that our hearts might not be as satisfied or content as we would have ourselves or others believe. Rather, the chase to have it all might just reveal a heart that is discontent and dissatisfied.

---

9. Anna Patty, 'Mindfulness takes over the corporate world', *Sydney Morning Herald,* 30 October 2015 (accessed 18 July 2017), smh.com.au/business/workplace-relations/mindfulness-takes-over-the-corporate-world-20151029-gkm4mo.html.

Why do we keep adding more and more and more to our diaries? Why do we keep adding more and more and more to our to-do lists? Why do our holiday plans suddenly take on a life of their own and end up far bigger than we anticipated? Why isn't what I am currently doing enough?

Could it be that our hearts are not truly satisfied? The latest work-place success, current house, level of fitness or entertainment experience hasn't filled that hole. And so we add another thing out of the mistaken belief that having it will satisfy us and make us content.

The area where I am most prone to do this is my work life. I already have more than enough good things on my to-do list to keep me going for a very long time. But I just keep on adding more. Why? In my better moments it is because I think of a task that could serve and benefit others. But I know that my to-do list is also filled with items that stem from a dissatisfied heart – a heart that believes achieving or accomplishing one thing more might fill it up.

This pursuit can be deadly. Not one but three of the Gospels record these words from Jesus: 'What good will it be for a man if he gains the whole world, yet forfeits his soul?' (Matthew 16:26; see also Mark 8:36, Luke 9:25). When we seek to gain the whole world and have it all, we run the deadly and dangerous risk of attaining what we want yet losing what really matters. FOMO, the 'fear of missing out', will be the death us.

A mistaken and proud heart

The pressure to have it all may also reveal a mistaken view of yourself. Perhaps you have fallen into the trap of thinking that you are able to cope with a work, family, social, church load that is, quite frankly, humanly impossible. It's a faulty view, and one that reflects an underlying pride.

From the first pages of the Bible, humans have suffered from a particular sickness: trying to be like God (Genesis 3:5). The one who made the world and rules the universe can do everything. 'Is anything too hard for the Lord?' is the rhetorical question in Genesis 18:14, the implied answer being, no! He is omnipotent, all-powerful. But in our worst moments we mistakenly think that we are too. We believe that we can do all things. We forget that we are finite, that we 'are a mist that appears for a little while and then vanishes' (James 4:14). We grow proud.

We know that there are so many good things that we could do, another useful task, helpful deed, serving act we could take on in the workplace, the home, the neighbourhood or at church. The question is not whether there are good things to do or not, it is how much can one person handle. And the answer is, only so much!

Confession time: this is a particular problem of mine. As we think about the pressure to have it all, I'm the number one culprit when it comes to trying to have it all in my work life. This chapter, unlike some of the others in this book, is written for me first and foremost! Most of the work-related pressure I experience does not come from colleagues or the people that I interact with; most of it is self-inflicted. It comes from taking on more tasks than I can possibly handle because I mistakenly think that I can manage. And for short periods I *do* cope. Then the weight becomes too heavy and it all comes crashing down.

Journalist Oliver Burkeman puts it well: 'We feel a social pressure to 'do it all', at work and at home, but that's not just really difficult; it's a mathematical impossibility'.[10] We are finite creatures and we cannot have and do it all. How often our proud hearts make the mistake of thinking that we can.

---

10. Oliver Burkeman, 'Why you feel busy all the time (when you're actually not)', *BBC*, 12 September 2016 (accessed 18 July 2017), bbc.com/future/story/20160909-why-you-feel-busy-all-the-time-when-youre-actually-not

A forgetful heart

What if I told you that, in spite of what I've just said, you actually *could* have it all? That one day you *will* have it all? Not the 'all' that you might want for yourself, but the 'all' that really matters and will truly satisfy you. This is precisely the hope for the Christian.

Our culture suffers from what philosopher Charles Taylor calls living in the 'immanent frame'.[11] That is, we think that what we can see, taste and touch is all that there is. What is right before me, what is immanent, is the sum total of this universe. There is nothing outside of the physical world; there is nothing to come after this life. If I am to experience pleasure and satisfaction, I must do so immediately. This is the reason for the success of a well-known book series that lists the 1001 books, films, albums and holidays that you must read, see, listen to and do 'before you die'. If there is nothing more than what lies before us, we've got to do it all now!

But the Christian person knows that this is not all there is. There is a heaven and there is a hell. There is a spiritual world of angels and the devil. There is a God. And there is a life to come, with him.

So a 'have it all' mindset can also stem from a forgetful heart. We forget that this is not all there is. We live like the world around us in the immanent frame, thinking that we must have everything *now* if we're going to have it all.

God: The solution outside

With heart problems like these, merely looking within cannot help us handle the pressure to have it all. 'The heart is deceitful above all

---

11. Charles Taylor, *A Secular Age*, (Cambridge, MA: Harvard University Press, 2007), 542.

things. Who can truly understand it?' (Jeremiah 17:9). Only the one who made it. Only the one who can heal it. The solution is found in encountering afresh the God who is all-satisfying, all-powerful and eternal.

Finding contentment in the all-satisfying God

Early Christian theologian Augustine famously wrote, 'Thou hast made us for thyself, O Lord, and our heart is restless until it finds its rest in Thee'.[12] Our restless, dissatisfied hearts will never be satisfied by having it all, yet we put ourselves under enormous pressure trying to 'gain the world' (Matthew 16:26). Our hearts will only ever find rest, contentment and satisfaction in the One who made us, the all-satisfying God (Hebrews 13:5).

So when you are next tempted by the pursuit to have it all, instead join with the psalmist in saying, 'Whom have I in heaven but you, and earth has nothing I desire besides you. My flesh and my heart may fail, but God is the strength of my heart and my portion forever' (Psalm 73:25–26). All the good things that we might pursue can never compare to the God who is our portion forever. Earth has nothing that can satisfy like him. He is even better than life itself.

And join with the psalmist in praying, 'Teach me your ways, O Lord, and I will walk in your truth, give me an undivided heart, that I may fear your name' (Psalm 86:11). Our hearts are pulled in many different directions by many good things. But the psalmist prays for 'an undivided heart', a heart that is completely given to God, walking in his ways and fearing him. The solution to our dissatisfied hearts is an undivided heart, satisfied in God.

It really is a matter of life and death. For why does Jesus warn that gaining the whole world, having it all, could cost us our souls? Perhaps it is because when we are gaining it all we leave no room for

---

12. Augustine of Hippo, *Confessions*, Book 1, chapter 1.

the One we really need for life. We risk missing out on being truly satisfied.

Embracing this truth frees us from the need to chase every experience, every opportunity, every possession. Because even if we do not 'have it all', we do have the greatest treasure of all – God.

Relying on the all-powerful God

It's a truth taught to kids in church from an early age: 'My God is so big, so strong and so mighty, there's nothing my God cannot do'. Perhaps as adults we need to sing and remind ourselves of this truth regularly too – and alongside it, the truth that we cannot do everything.

Scripture reminds us over and over again that we are finite (Psalm 103:15–18; 1 Peter 1:24). On our own apart from Jesus we can do nothing (John 15:5). It is a mistake to think otherwise, but when we try to have it all we are not living as though this is true. There is only one who can do it all and have it all and he is the one who made us and sustains us. This truth humbles us and rebukes our pride.

Rather than trying to do and have everything, we need to prioritise. We need to do well those non-negotiable duties and responsibilities that we have. That might include a set list of tasks on a job description, or the responsibility of raising young children or caring for elderly family members – both sizeable, non-negotiable responsibilities and ones that will require us to say no to other good opportunities.

For me personally, recognising that life has seasons (Ecclesiastes 3:1–8) has helped me to learn to say no. Right now I am in a season of raising young children with my wife. It's a starkly different season to being single. And I imagine that having grown-up children who have moved out of home will be a different season again. My current season involves certain responsibilities that mean I can't say yes to other good opportunities. I often remind myself, sometimes through gritted teeth, that 'there is a time for everything, and a season for every activity under the heavens' (Ecclesiastes 3:1). There is a time to raise kids. There is also a time to take roles requiring extended work travel – and, for me, that time is not now!

Remembering our finitude, accepting that life has seasons and resting in our all-satisfying God will humble and shape us. This truth helps us grow in trust and contentment so that we can stop putting ourselves under unnecessary pressure by trying to have it all.

Hoping in the eternal God

Despite what our culture might tell us, this world is not all there is. There is more than what I can just see, taste, touch and experience now. A new heavens and a new earth is coming where we will 'have it all' – well, the 'all' that really matters.

'Then I saw "a new heaven and a new earth", for the first heaven and the first earth had passed away, and there was no longer any sea. I saw the Holy City, the new Jerusalem, coming down out of heaven from God, prepared as a bride beautifully dressed for her husband. And I heard a loud voice from the throne saying, "Look! God's dwelling place is now among the people, and he will dwell with them. They will be his people and God himself will be with them and be their God. He will wipe every tear from their eyes. There will be no more death or mourning or crying or pain, for the old order of things has passed away"' (Revelation 21:1–4).

When I hear these verses taught or explained, the emphasis is frequently placed on the part that says, 'no more death or mourning or crying or pain' (21:4). Indeed, this verse is a tremendous comfort and hope for the Christian person, especially in the face of difficulty in this life. But I wonder if the more significant hope that these verses include, certainly the one which helps us handle the pressure to have it all, is found one verse earlier: 'He will dwell with them' (21:3). This is a picture of what was lost at Eden, dwelling in the perfect presence of our all-satisfying God. Being in God's presence – what more could we want? To dwell with him is to have it all. This is why the Apostle Paul can write, 'for me to live is Christ, and to die is gain' (Philippians 1:21).

You won't have it all in this lifetime: I can almost guarantee it. You'll miss out on a certain experience. You won't get to travel to a particular place. You won't be able to take on all the opportunities that you'd love to in the workplace. There will be sore disappointments and dreams that slip away. Hard though this may be to stomach, in the face of eternity and in the presence of the all-satisfying God these missed opportunities will cease to matter.

In the meantime, while we wait for that final fulfilment, we practice 'the daily discipline of ongoing relinquishment'.[13] We say no, we give up, we settle for less. We remove good things from our lives that are nevertheless symptomatic of us trying to have it all. One small way that I do this is by going through my to-do list once a week and removing items from it – many of them good things, but things I know I'll never be able to do because I can't do it all or have it all.

Remembering these truths can be hard in our world of the immediate and immanent. But forgetting them can become even harder, as we place unnecessary pressure on ourselves to have it all, now. Missing out in this life is okay.

13. Paul Stevens and Alvin Ung, *Taking Your Soul to Work: Overcoming the Nine Deadly Sins of the Workplace*, (Grand Rapids: Eerdmans, 2010), 92.

HEART AND HABIT CHANGE

Which of the three heart problems most resonates with you: a dissatisfied and discontent heart, a mistaken and proud heart, or a forgetful heart? Why?

1. If it is a dissatisfied and discontent heart, consider memorising a verse like Psalm 73:25–26 and reciting it to yourself or others at the start or end of the day.

2. If it is a mistaken and proud heart, take a moment to reflect on the season of life you are in. What might you be trying to do that is possible in another season but unrealistic in this one? Can you let it go for now?

3. If it is a forgetful heart, perhaps add something to your to-do list: a weekly time when you practice the 'discipline of ongoing relinquishment'. Set aside 15–30 minutes at the start or end of each week to take items off your to-do list.

A controversial suggestion for families

If missing out in this life is okay, then let me make one final, perhaps controversial, suggestion especially for those in the 'married with children' season of life. If you are feeling under enormous pressure, I urge you to sit down with your spouse (after the kids are in bed, or on a rare occasion out alone together) and seriously ask yourselves, 'To what degree is our pressure caused by an attempt to have it all?'

Ask questions about the nature and amount of employment that you might be pursuing. Is one spouse working exorbitant hours because they don't want to miss out on career recognition? Are both of you in paid employment because you don't want to miss out on a certain size and style of house in a particular suburb, or that new model of car or extravagant holiday? Be honest with yourselves and each other.

For me it's not the pursuit of a certain lifestyle, but the pursuit of more and more achievements, that provides the greater temptation. Because of my ambition, I keep slipping back into work patterns that were manageable when I was single (and even when it was just my wife and I) but now with kids the pressure is not sustainable for my family. Talking with (and observing) other men in the same season of life as me, I know that I'm not alone. There are lots of us with families still trying to have it all in our work, regardless of whether our spouse is working or not. Kids have come along but there has been no real effort to adjust work travel or other commitments. Or we justify exorbitant hours with the claim it's being done to 'provide for the family'. Men, ask yourselves, are you trying to have it all in the workplace at a cost to your family?

For other families, maybe it is the pressure of a certain lifestyle that has driven both spouses into paid employment. Don't get me wrong – I know that for some families there are very good and absolutely necessary reasons for both spouses to be in paid employment. But for others of us, we need to ask the question: are we under so much pressure as a family due to necessity or because we want to achieve a certain lifestyle? Could the pressure that we are under as a family be alleviated by settling for less for our kids and ourselves?

As you discuss these questions together, ask what combination of employment would enable you as a family to best love God and serve your neighbour. It might mean dropping to part-time employment, whether each spouse works three days a week or one for four days, the other for one. Or it might mean shifting to one spouse in full-time paid employment, and the other in full-time management of household responsibilities for a season.

Please don't think that I'm suggesting that it is automatically the female who should make household responsibilities their primary work. When it comes to who is the 'chief family breadwinner', the Christian faith gives us great freedom. As one writer explains, 'Scripture does not give us a list of things men and women must and must not do . . . rigid cultural gender roles have no Biblical warrant'.[14]

In our twelve years of marriage there have been times where my wife provided almost all of the finances for our family through her employment, and times when I have carried most of that responsibility. At one stage, twelve months after the birth of our first child, we each spent three days in paid employment as well as sharing the role of primary carer for our child (and that season forever changed how I think about raising kids). At other stages I've made decisions that were honestly pretty self-serving, guided more by a pressure to have it all in the workplace – so I certainly haven't always got it right!

Other couples I know have adjusted the combination of employment that they have in order to choose less ambitious career paths, relieving some of the pressure that they are under in order to be better able to love God and serve their neighbour. One Christian couple I know with three young children recently made a fairly major decision just like this. Both were highly successful in their respective careers. But with both of their roles requiring them to move cities to progress in their career, they sat down to consider some of the questions I've suggested here. Should one or both of them settle for a less ambitious career path? Should one be in full-time employment while the other worked mostly around the home, developing a career on the side? Should both continue to pursue full-time paid employment and find a way to juggle the travel responsibilities of both?

---

14. Timothy Keller, *The Meaning of Marriage*, (London: Hodder & Stoughton, 2013), 186.

After much prayer and talking with others, they decided that the wife had a unique opportunity to be a strong, Christian, female leader in an organisation dominated by a very different culture. To facilitate this, her husband took on the primary care role at home with a view to developing a business on the side as the kids grew older. This solution was, they felt, the most strategic way to serve God and avoid the overwhelm that would come from the two of them in full-time employment roles. It wasn't an easy decision, and it doesn't mean life is free of pressure for them now, but it was one that could only be made when they were free from the pressure to have it all in this lifetime.

Freedom from the pressure to have it all

The pressure to have it all is a real pressure. It pervades our culture. But oftentimes, as we've seen, it is primarily self-imposed. We can choose not to pursue 'having it all'.

That won't always be easy in a world that is telling us otherwise, and we will need to keep reminding ourselves of the all-satisfying, all-powerful, eternal God we know and can rest in. But when we do live that way it is wonderfully freeing. To be free from the pursuit of trying to have it all is truly liberating. It is to experience the kind of freedom from burdens that Jesus promises those who take on his easy yoke (Matthew 11:30).

But not all the pressure we experience is self-imposed. Not all of it is internally driven or our own fault. Rather, we're part of a working world that imposes enormous pressure upon us. We'll take a look at that pressure next.

HOW TO HANDLE... THE PRESSURE OF EVER-PRESENT WORK

It was four days after Christmas. I was staying at my parents' house going through boxes of my old belongings when my eldest daughter, who was three at the time, reached into one and pulled out a cassette tape. 'What's this, Daddy?' she asked. 'That is a tape,' I responded. *And you just made me feel old*, I thought quietly to myself. It feels like only yesterday I was collecting and cataloguing cassette tapes, and now my daughter holds one up in wonder at what it is.

The speed at which technology changes is rapid, and at times overwhelming. Recently I took my iPhone in for an upgrade and the sales assistant's eyes opened wide when he saw the model I was still using. I'd had this supposedly prehistoric phone for two years.

Technology is always developing, and this is largely a good thing. Improvements in science, medicine, communication and travel can provide great blessings. But it is often the case that we embrace technological advancements and only later reflect on their impact upon us. That's why, in recent years, many people have begun asking questions about the way changes to technology are impacting how, when and where we work, and whether all of them are for the best.

Changing the how, when and where of work

It's obvious that changes to technology have had a revolutionary impact on work in recent decades – a revolution that some suggest is even greater than the Industrial Revolution. We are now deep in the Information Revolution.

Not too many generations ago, most work was of a manufacturing or farming nature. That kind of work had inbuilt limits: you could only farm for certain hours of the day, when the sun was up; and as much as you might have liked to get ahead on next month's projects, you simply could not harvest the crops until they were ready. Even manufacturing work had some built-in constraints; you could only make as many products as you had the resources for.[15]

But the working world has changed. Many of us now do what we described in the introduction as 'knowledge work', the kind of work that puts information together rather than physical materials. Architects, software developers, lawyers, academics, accountants and writers – our main capital is not timber or wheat but information and knowledge. And in one sense that is an infinite resource. If I, or my organisation, can think it or dream it, then potentially we can do it.

Add to this the coinciding developments in technology, and there's a growing sense that my work (and the potential to do just a little bit more of it) is always with me. I can scribble down a few more ideas on my laptop, or keep working on that design on my tablet while in bed. I can reach into my pocket and send another email at any hour of the day. Tony Crabbe, in his book *Busy: How to Thrive in a World of*

15. Burkeman, 'Why you feel busy all the time (when you're actually not)'.

Too Much, describes this as being in an 'infinite world' that combines both no end of possibilities and no escape from them.[16]

Not all these changes are negative. The freedom and flexibility to work anywhere and at any time, when managed well, can be wonderful for increased productivity and employee happiness. Some employers are beginning to realise this, encouraging their employees to enter the office for a few hours only, in the middle of the day for meetings; they are otherwise free to work wherever, whenever, just as long as the job gets done.[17] The focus for these managers is on 'the mission of the job rather than the time in the chair',[18] leading to greater engagement, productivity and happiness for their staff.

The Information Revolution also brings the return of something that was lost for many in the Industrial Revolution - the joy of creativity. 'The Information Age and the present Age of Creativity perhaps offer more scope for creativity as work moves from repetitive tasks to creative interventions, a kind of artisanship done in the imagination and mind.'[19] The Information Revolution has replaced some of the repetitive tasks of the industrial age with work that is more innovative and imaginative in nature, giving work the potential to be fun, even joyful.

For all the potential positives, however, the combination of endless work possibilities and no apparent escape from that work is placing most of us under enormous pressure. According to one recent survey, 46% of workers in Australia say technology makes them feel like they are 'always on'. 'When reflecting on the impacts of the changing workplace, respondents were largely in agreement

---

16. Tony Crabbe, *Busy: How to Thrive in a World of Too Much*, (London: Piatkus Books, 2014), 9.
17. For example, see Caitlin Fitzsimmons, 'Bosses need to catch up: the traditional nine-to-five-work day is dead', 30 November 2016 (accessed 18 July 2017), smh.com.au/comment/bosses-need-to-catch-up-the-traditional-ninetofivework-day-is-dead-20161129-gszzyq.html.
18. Schulte, *Overwhelmed*, 88.
19. Stevens and Ung, *Taking Your Soul to Work*, 73.

that advances in technology have not, in the main, freed them from work, but made work *a constant pressure* in their lives.'[20]

Slaves to the system

It's little surprise, then, that 'busy' is one of the most frequent responses I hear to the question 'How are you?' (and one of the responses I'm commonly tempted to give!)

But are we really any busier than previous generations? While there is no disputing the changing nature of work and its ever-present nature, the reality is that most of us aren't actually working longer hours than previous generations. 'The total time people are working – whether paid or otherwise – has not increased . . . in recent decades. Modern parents who worry they're spending insufficient time with their children spend significantly more of it than those in generations past'.[21]

So why do I feel so busy if I'm not actually working longer hours? For some, part of the reason might be the juggle of husband and wife who, as parents, are both in paid employment. Each are working regular days, but one starts later to drop the kids at school, another finishes earlier to pick the kids up, and the day becomes stretched. So the individual hours aren't greater, but the days are longer.

But the ever-present nature of work might also explain our feeling of busyness, a sense that we are 'always on'. The five-minute interruption from a colleague's text message in the evening, or the quick email that is sent before leaving for the office in the morning, add to our sense of always working. We can never truly get away from work so we feel constantly busy, and 'living in an always-on tech-

---

20. afuturethatworks.org.au/reports (accessed 19 July 2017). Italics mine. For millennials, that figure rises to 54%.
21. Burkeman, 'Why you feel busy all the time (when you're actually not)'.

nological haze leads to mental exhaustion'.[22] Work is ever present – a constant pressure.

I wonder if sometimes all this pressure feels like slavery? The constant sense of being available, the 24/7 work cycle, the after-hours ping of a text message about work. It's like a modern day form of slavery where we are bound to a demanding workplace system. Unlike the pressure to have it all, which is oftentimes self-imposed, the pressure of ever-present work feels like something we can't escape from.

It perhaps wasn't too different for the Jews of Jesus' age, who knew what it was like to be part of a demanding system – a demanding religious system that Jesus describes in terms of slavery, a system with leaders who 'tie up heavy, cumbersome loads and put them on other people's shoulders, but they themselves are not willing to lift a finger to move them' (Matthew 23:4).

This slavery imagery Jesus employs would have resonated deeply with his Jewish audience, harking back to their *physical* slavery in Egypt (Exodus 1:8–11). Now Jesus picks up on that slavery imagery, not to speak of the past, but to shed light on the then-present *religious* slavery the Jewish people found themselves under. And like many of us, they were going along with the system they found themselves a part of, just living with the pressure of it.

In his book *Sabbath as Resistance: Saying No to a Culture of Now*, Old Testament theologian Walter Brueggemann reflects on today's working world as being like a system of slavery. The cruel slave drivers are the gods of this age – commodity and consumption – and they drive our workplaces at a cruel pace. Brueggemann writes,

> These gods of commoditization for the most part go unchallenged in our world. As a result, their exploitative systems go unchallenged and unnoticed. The

22. Schulte, *Overwhelmed*, 26.

> abuse becomes normal. Restlessness is unexceptional. Anxiety is a given, and violence is unexamined as 'the cost of doing business'. It is all a virtual reality in which we become narcotized into a system that seems to be a given rather than a construction.[23]

Rarely do we stop and question the system that we are a part of. We take it as a given that this is simply what is required to live and work in the Information Age.

A better kind of slavery

But Jesus speaks into our context, too, and offers hope. Aware of Israel's *physical* slavery in the past, and their present *religious* slavery, he says, 'Come to me all you who are weary and burdened, and I will give you rest. Take my yoke upon you and learn from me, for I am gentle and humble in heart, and you will find rest for your souls. For my yoke is easy and my burden is light' (Matthew 11:28–30).

To the weary and exhausted, have more refreshing words ever been spoken? Rest. Gentleness. Humility. The very words themselves make me feel calmer!

The context of these words is that Jesus has just spoken about his relationship with his Father, explaining that if you want to know the Father then you need to know him, the Son (11:25–27). Then he makes this invitation: 'Come to me . . . and I will give you rest'.

Spiritual rest or physical rest?

Before we unpack what Jesus means, we need to address an important question. We began this chapter talking about a *physical* kind of slavery to a demanding workplace system. But in this passage Jesus is addressing a *spiritual* kind of slavery to a demanding

23. Walter Brueggemann, *Sabbath as Resistance: Saying No to a Culture of Now*, (Louisville: Westminster/John Knox, 2014), 17.

religious system. Primarily, the kind of rest that he is offering in these verses is not physical, but spiritual. So does this passage have anything to say to our problem? Yes, and here's how.

A classic New Testament passage about rest is found in Hebrews 4. There, the author holds out a promise of entering ultimate rest to followers of Jesus (4:1–11). It's a picture of being back in relationship with God – kind of like a return to Eden (Genesis 1–2), but better. Right relationship with God is the true and ultimate rest, and we know how we enter into that rest – through Jesus' death and resurrection. This is why his yoke is good news for those under a demanding religious system. Rather than having to work to get ourselves right with God, Jesus says, 'Bind yourselves to me, because I have done all the work necessary for you to be right with God. Come to me all you who are weary and burdened, and I will give you spiritual rest'.

But – and this is a big but – it's a mistake to separate physical rest from spiritual rest. The New Testament sees a very tight connection between the two. For example, this passage in Matthew about spiritual rest is followed immediately by a passage about physical rest on the Sabbath (Matthew 12:1–8). Physical and spiritual rest are inseparable; oftentimes our physical rest-*less*-ness is an outworking of a spiritual rest-*less*-ness. We're busy because we're trying to prove ourselves, or earn the approval of others, or keep things under control, all of which have spiritual problems at their root that impact us physically.[24] Similarly, large parts of our demanding workplace system might have the same spiritual problems at their root, so to address one type of rest in our lives, spiritual rest, is to begin to address the other, physical rest. The two go hand in hand.

So, Jesus' words do apply to our own modern day form of slavery. 'Take my yoke upon you,' he encourages us. The yoke

---

24. For more on this see Tim Chester's excellent book, *A Busy Christian's Guide to Busyness*, (Nottingham: IVP, 2011). Chester goes through a series of spiritual problems that might lie beneath our physical restlessness.

was an article of slavery, something which bound a person to another. And Jesus says to those bound to a demanding system, not 'free yourselves from all bindings', but 'bind yourselves instead to me'.

How is that good news for the weary and exhausted? It's good news because, unlike the demanding yoke of slavery that Jesus' listeners were under, unlike the demanding yoke of slavery that *you* are under, Jesus' yoke in comparison is easy and his burden is light. Jesus does not say, 'Come to me . . . once you've fulfilled these requirements, or cleaned up your act', but simply, 'Come to me. I know your burdens. I know your weariness. I know your exhaustion from trying to fulfil the demands of the religious system that you are under, trying to fulfil the demands of the workplace system that you are part of. Come to me and find a more restful way under my guidance'.

And how can we trust that Jesus' yoke is easy? Because of his character. Jesus explains, 'learn from me, for I am gentle and humble in heart'. For Jesus' original audience, humility and gentleness stood in stark contrast to the proud and ostentatious system of the Pharisees. And it stands in stark contrast to the proud and ostentatious workplace system of our day. Jesus invites us out from under the burdensome slavery of our working world to learn how to live differently under his loving yoke. Let's look at what this 'learning with Jesus' could look like for us.

Acts of resistance

Jesus' words sound refreshing, but you may wonder just how they can help you to cope with this demanding workplace system – the pressure of ever-present work. In this section, I want to show that 'binding ourselves to Jesus' or being under his yoke is not a fluffy spiritual concept but an immensely practical one.

First, it's vital to get our thinking right when it comes to rest. If spiritual rest and physical rest are deeply connected, then right thinking about spiritual rest is key to right living when it comes to physical rest. Knowing that in Jesus we have true rest frees us from trying to work to prove ourselves through our work. Just like Jesus' original audience, we too can rest in him who has done all that is necessary for salvation (we don't need to work to prove ourselves to anyone) and in whose sovereign hands we rest (we don't need to work to keep things under control). He is our ultimate master – not the demanding workplace system.

How does this change how I handle the pressure of ever-present work? I think the title of Walter Brueggemann's book that I mentioned earlier gives us a big clue – *Sabbath as Resistance*. We live as people who are ultimately bound to Jesus, yet we still live in a world where we have to function within the demanding workplace system. This means that at times we might need to undertake 'acts of resistance'. Sometimes to live Jesus' way of restfulness, ultimately bound to his yoke, will require us to push back against a system that is seeking to bind us to itself.

Here are some possible acts of resistance that could be helpful as you seek to make it known to the world that you're ultimately under Jesus' yoke. (I offer these as suggestions, not heavy loads to place on your shoulders!)

Practice humility and gentleness

Binding ourselves to Jesus means binding ourselves to one who is 'gentle and humble' (Matthew 11:29). As I said earlier, there is something about those words that I find deeply calming. And I don't think that is an accident. Because if you've ever practised gentleness and humility you'll know it is a more restful way to live.

Jesus offers himself to us as the 'gentle and humble' master. Now, the New Testament makes it plain that those who follow Jesus and are filled with his Spirit become more and more like him, including becoming people of gentleness and humility. In proud and ostentatious workplaces, living gently and humbly will also become a point of difference, at times even an act of resistance, because gentleness is not a common feature of modern workplaces. Chances are you've never encountered a job description that required it of you. On the contrary, a requirement of many workplaces is that employees do the opposite – refuse to take no for an answer, throw weight around and so 'get things done'.

Yet gentleness is to be a defining characteristic of the Christian person. Elsewhere in the New Testament it is cited as evidence that someone is living by the Spirit (Galatians 5:23). We are to pursue it (1 Timothy 6:11) and clothe ourselves in it (Colossians 3:12). And this gentleness is not only to be directed towards those colleagues that we like but also those who oppose us (2 Timothy 2:25). We are to 'be gentle toward everyone' (Titus 3:2). Gentleness is to shape our interactions with unbelievers when they ask us about the hope that we have (1 Peter 3:15).

You could think of gentleness as 'humility in action'. In the New Testament the word that is often translated as 'gentleness' is in some cases translated as humility.[25] In at least two cases, humility and gentleness are seen as inseparable (2 Corinthians 10:1; Ephesians 4:2). Jesus places them side by side in this passage in Matthew also. Gentleness is, perhaps, the defining characteristic of a humble person.

This doesn't mean that a gentle person will never be firm. Paul can write to the Corinthians, 'By the humility and gentleness of Christ I urge you' (2 Corinthians 10:1). But it may mean that when we put forward a strong opinion strongly, we do so with a willingness to be persuaded otherwise. We will take no for an answer. We won't fight for our way to the bitter end.

---

25. See for example James 1:21; 3:13 in the NIV.

What has this got to do with restfulness and handling the pressure of ever-present work? Well a strange thing happens when you practice gentleness and humility. You actually begin to *feel* more restful, relaxed, at peace and calm. Life doesn't feel so pressured, demanding and exhausting when you learn to live like the one who is 'gentle and humble'. Being forceful and proud is tiring; being gentle and humble is restful. It also opens the way up to other acts of resistance.

Say no

Humility will mean that you no longer have to say yes to everything: partly because you're able to let opportunities pass you by so that others might shine instead of you, and partly because you're resting in Christ and not your own labours. Learning the way of gentleness and humility allows you to gently turn down requests because you don't need to prove yourself. You're no longer trying to please a certain slave master because you have the approval of a new master.

We might baulk at this in part, because we rightly want to serve others. Some of us find it very hard to say no. But being a servant doesn't mean needing to say yes to every request in the office – especially if our yes is born out of a desire to satisfy an old slave master. Check yourself when you're tempted to say yes to everything. Why are you saying yes? Are you simply trying to impress others or prove yourself? Or is this a situation where you have no choice in the matter? If so, take the task on and ask your gentle and humble Lord to sustain you. But if there *is* a choice and you are already overwhelmed, embrace the freedom that comes with being yoked to Jesus and say no.

Turn off from work

One of the simplest ways of handling the pressure of ever-present work is to literally turn off devices that keep you bound to that system when you are no longer physically in the office or required to be working. And yes, seriously, you can do this!

A big lie of the demanding workplace system is that the world will stop turning if you stop working. But for the one bound to the sovereign Lord who controls all things, you know this not to be true. Therefore, you are free to release yourself from the bindings of the demanding workplace system – at least for a few hours of a day or week.

Perhaps you've heard this practice described as a 'technology Sabbath', the idea of turning off devices for a period of time each week. It's a concept that's becoming increasingly popular. Google 'technology Sabbath' and you'll discover a wealth of helpful articles on the topic. But Christians have something that is missing from much of this wisdom: the spiritual purpose and resources to regularly embrace such a Sabbath. We know that we are ultimately bound to Christ, not bound to our workplace cultures and systems, so we truly have a freedom to switch off regularly. When the demanding workplace system is still your ultimate master it will keep pressuring you to give up on such a Sabbath.

What might a technology Sabbath look like? For me it means turning off my phone when I arrive home from work in the evening and keeping it off until my kids are in bed. It's only a couple of hours, and if there is a family emergency those in the know are aware of how they might make urgent contact. I turn off at this time for two reasons: first, so that I can switch off from work for a couple of important hours with my kids, and second, so that my kids don't see me bound to my phone. I want to model to them what it looks like to be bound to Jesus, which is very hard to do when my head is in my phone while they're trying to talk to me. (Yes, I've been there too many times.)

Added to this evening Sabbath, I also aim for a weekend Sabbath where I turn off my phone and laptop from sundown Friday night to sunup Sunday morning. There's nothing inherently spiritual about these particular hours, although it is the traditional Jewish Sabbath. It's simply a good time for me to switch off and it's what works best for my family. You might choose the same pattern or a different pattern. The important thing is that we learn to switch off as a way of loosening some of the ties to a demanding system – a practical way to remind ourselves that our workplace is not our ultimate master.

Don't always choose the most efficient way

One of the features of the demanding workplace is the emphasis placed on efficiency. I've already admitted to my love for efficiency in the previous chapter, and those who know me well know that it's something I value highly. But efficiency often comes at the expense of relationships; 'efficiency savings' usually means people losing jobs. Efficiency also lacks gentleness. On the contrary, inefficiency often helps develop relationships.

So when the opportunity is available, choose the inefficient way as an act of resistance. You'll find that it slows you down both mentally and physically, helping you to feel more rested. One way that I try to practice this act of resistance is by taking a longer commute on occasion, whether by public transport or riding my bike, instead of taking the absolute quickest way to get to work. This act gives me an opportunity at the start of the day to reflect, oftentimes on the rest that I have in Jesus and what it might mean to live bound to him. Another way I do this is by not always getting my coffee as a take-away, instead taking five or ten minutes to sit and drink it at the cafe. Not only does it mean I get to know the staff (inefficiency helping to foster relationships) but it's another chance to slow down, take stock and move gently.

Perhaps you could walk an extra block to get your lunch. Or even just get out of your workplace at lunchtime to walk around the block! Again, doing that inefficient act opens up the possibility to do it with a colleague and so foster a relationship. Whatever you choose to do, find some small and creative ways to resist the dominant culture and be regularly inefficient.

HABIT CHANGE

1. Which of the four acts of resistance (practicing gentleness, saying no, switching off and being inefficient) did you find most appealing? Make a commitment to practice one act of resistance in the week ahead – place a note in your diary or to-do list.

2. Which act/s felt impossible to do? Why? Are the obstacles real or perceived/self-imposed?

3. Gentleness is a hallmark of a Spirit-filled and empowered life (Galatians 5:23). It doesn't just happen by trying really hard. Consider resolving to pray about gentleness each morning for the next ten days.

What to do when there is no escape

I know what some of you might be thinking at this point. Yes, Jesus is my ultimate master. Yes, I'm seeking to learn to live his way of gentleness and humility. Yes, acts of resistance will sometimes be useful for both demonstrating that he is my ultimate master and relieving some of the pressure of ever-present work. But Andrew . . . you don't know my workplace and my boss.

And my answer to that is, you're right. I don't know first-hand the overwhelming pressure that you are under. I don't know your boss – the one you feel is impossible to say no to. I don't know how hard you have already been trying to switch off from ever-present work, but to no avail. I don't know. But your master does. And he has something to say to you even in this kind of situation.

Up to this point in the chapter we have been exploring ways to relieve and resist some of the pressure of ever-present work. And this is a good and right thing. There is only so much pressure that we can each handle. But in reflecting on how to handle pressure there is a critical caveat we need to consider. That is, that not all pressure is bad.

As I said in the introduction, pressure denotes the idea of being squeezed, pushed, or pressed in by something or someone. But just like applying pressure to an orange produces something positive – juice – so a good amount of pressure in our lives can also be a positive thing.

Pressure as a good thing

Health professionals are certainly aware of this. Doctor Steve Midgley writes about the 'stress response curve', where just the right amount of pressure produces a positive result. 'Our performance improves in line with the motivational demand upon us . . . as the pressure on us rises, so does our performance. That, for example is why athletes regularly produce performances in an Olympic finals which they would never manage in training.'[26]

But this is not just wisdom from health professionals. The Bible takes this view of pressure also. Our culture resists the idea that suffering, difficulty and pressure can be useful, viewing them as things to be avoided at all costs. Scripture, however, shows that

---

26. Dr Steve Midgley in Christopher Ash, *Zeal Without Burnout*, (New Malden, UK: Good Book Company, 2016), 117.

suffering leads to glory, and difficulty, hardship and pressure are means that God uses to refine us.

Romans 5:3–4 puts this most plainly: 'We glory in our sufferings, because we know suffering produces perseverance; perseverance, character; and character, hope.' There is a place for 'glorying' in our sufferings, difficulty and pressure because of the way that God might use these for our good. As New York pastor Timothy Keller puts it, 'A lump of coal under pressure becomes a diamond. And the suffering of a person in Christ only turns you into somebody gorgeous.'[27]

So when it feels like you are under pressure from that which you cannot entirely escape, resentment is not your only option. Instead, you can accept and welcome some pressure for the good that it might do, the 'priceless grace'[28] that such pressure can be and the way that God might use it to refine your heart. You will only learn patience when you're put in a situation where you are tested by impatience. You will only learn gentleness when you're in the midst of busyness and tempted by efficiency at the cost of relationships. You will only learn perseverance when you're stuck in something you have to persevere through. It's worth having a bit of pressure sometimes to help us learn perseverance, isn't it?

It's a great thing if we can accept the idea that pressure can do us some good. American author John Piper writes, 'I do live under a lot of pressure . . . but I don't begrudge that. I think deadlines and pressure are the most productive things in the world. If you try to run away from stress, run away from pressure, run away from deadlines, you'll probably be a relaxed do-nothing.'[29]

---

27. Timothy Keller, *Walking with God Through Pain and Suffering*, (New York: Dutton, 2013), 181.
28. Jon Bloom, 'The Priceless Grace of Pressure', 8 August 2014, accessed 19 July 2017, desiringgod.org/articles/the-priceless-grace-of-pressure
29. John Piper, 'What Do You Do To Relax and Unwind?', 2 February 2010 (accessed July 19 2017), desiringgod.org/interviews/what-do-you-do-to-relax-and-unwind.

Some pressure can refine character and bring focus to work. Let's embrace it!

The witness of helplessness

When we find ourselves feeling helpless and overwhelmed by the pressure of ever-present work, there's also a powerful opportunity to demonstrate our desperate need for Jesus. Being in a place where we are beyond our means is not always a bad place to be. It is precisely the place where we start embracing the gospel, recognising we don't have all the resources, physically *and* spiritually, and that we need another.

In 2 Corinthians 12, the Apostle Paul recounts a cryptic event that concludes with him being given a 'thorn in the flesh' (12:7). Three times he pleads for God to take it away. But instead God says to him, 'My grace is sufficient for you, for my power is made perfect in weakness' (12:9). Therefore Paul concludes, 'I will boast about my weaknesses, so that Christ's power may rest on me' (12:9).

Paul rejoices in his suffering because when he is weak God's strength shines through. And it can be exactly the same for you when you're under pressure at work. Acknowledging weakness creates space for God's strength to shine. So join Paul in 'boasting' about your weakness – that the pressure of the demanding workplace system is at times too much. Admit it to your colleagues and employer. Be the kind of person who says, 'I don't know'. Chances are you're not the only one in your workplace who feels overwhelmed. But you might be the only one with the confidence to speak up, because you know that you have another master whose yoke you are under.

HEART CHANGE

1. What external pressures are you under at the moment that you can't escape from? Can you see any ways yet that God might be refining you through them? Don't worry if you can't – sometimes it is difficult to see this in the midst of the pressure (if at all!).

2. Consider memorising Romans 5:3–4 and reciting it to yourself when you are facing external pressures.

3. Do you find it easy to say 'I don't know' in the workplace? Why or why not? What heart issues might need to be addressed if you find it difficult to admit helplessness?

Resting: A 'bodily act of testimony'

In 1991, Sir James C. Brown wrote in *The Times* of London, 'We doctors in the treatment of nervous diseases are compelled to provide periods of rest. Some of these periods are, I think, only Sundays in arrears'.[30] If this was true in 1991, how much more today with the pressure of ever-present work?

Our colleagues are slaves to a demanding master. But there is a better way, a better master. And we know him. As we seek to live under his yoke, we learn to live his way of gentleness and humility, undertaking acts of resistance, embracing pressure for the good it can do and admitting when it is just too much. Not only do we help ourselves handle the pressure, we also bear witness to our colleagues, giving them a glimpse of our better master. Brueggemann describes

30. Quoted in Ash, *Zeal Without Burnout*, 117.

the practice of Sabbath as 'a bodily act of testimony'.[31] When we embrace spiritual rest in Christ and begin to let it shape our physical rest, we testify with our bodies, displaying to our colleagues something of what they are missing out on in not being yoked to Jesus. In a restless world, the restful stand out. Those who admit weakness allow the strength of God to shine through.

How can we possibly testify to a restless world of the rest that is found in Christ if we're constantly busy, restless people? The short answer is, we can't. So again, hear the words of Jesus: 'Come to me'. Come to him afresh. Keep coming to him each day. Keep learning what it means to live his restful way for your good, and the good of your colleagues.

---

31. Brueggemann, *Sabbath as Resistance*, 21.

HOW TO HANDLE... THE PRESSURE OF DIFFICULT WORKPLACE RELATIONSHIPS

Australian workers are on the move. 'Mobility' is one of the buzzwords used to describe our nation's workforce, with people hopping from job to job and career to career. At present, three years and four months is the average amount of time each of us will stay in a particular role before we're on the move again.[32] For twenty-five to thirty-five-year-olds, this drops to two years and eight months. On average, we'll each have seventeen different employers across the course of our paid working life and five different careers. One in five Australians has been in their current job for less than one year, while one in two has been in their role for less than five years.[33] My personal movement from job to job is not quite as frequent as this, but it's not too far off it!

32. 'Job Mobility in Australia', 18 June 2014 (accessed 19 July 2017), mccrindle.com.au/the-mccrindle-blog/job-mobility-in-australia
33. afuturethatworks.org.au/reports (accessed 19 July 2017).

When we observe this kind of phenomenon, a question comes to mind – why? Why are we changing jobs so frequently? The number one reason cited for this job movement is that people move to progress their careers. A move is an opportunity to learn new skills, to move up the corporate ladder, to tackle new challenges. In one study, 60% of Australian workers said that they find purpose and meaning in their work.[34] It's hardly surprising, then, that if you're not finding purpose and meaning in your current role you're likely to be on the move.

But there's a second reason frequently cited by those who have changed jobs, and this reason is best summarised as, 'I can't stand the people that I work with'. This is the pressure of difficult workplace relationships. As the title of one book puts it, especially for those in workplace leadership, 'management would be easy . . . if it weren't for the people'.[35]

Of course, work colleagues can be some of the best people in our lives. They, more than anyone else, can understand the pressures, challenges and joys of our daily work environment because they're in the thick of it with us. Our work colleagues appreciate the ups and downs of our particular jobs far better than some of our family members and closest friends. But when the people that we work with are difficult, it can make daily work miserable.

How should we handle difficult colleagues?

Rubbing up against difficult people at work is an experience that all of us understand to some degree. There's the lazy co-worker who takes credit for our work. Or the nightmare boss who blames you for their mistakes and rarely acknowledges your contribution. There's the childish employee who seems to have never grown up, the

---

34. afuturethatworks.org.au/reports (accessed 19 July 2017).
35. Patricia J. Addesso, *Management Would Be Easy . . . If It Weren't for the People*, (New York: AMACOM, 2001).

sleazy co-worker who is frankly unpleasant to be around, or that infuriating client who seems impossible to satisfy.

Relating to the people we work with can be the hardest part of the job! As one writer puts it, 'To be happier, more successful, and more stress-free at work, you only have to do two things well. You have to get the job done, and you have to handle the relationships with the people around you. Getting the job done tends to be the easy part'.[36]

And so how do many of us respond?

Strategy #1: Move away

As the mobility statistics above indicate, a common response to this kind of workplace pressure is simply to change jobs and move away. Rather than try and work through that difficult relationship, it feels easier, for those who have the option, to move workplace. According to one survey of 10,000 people, the person that we're most likely to want to move away from is the boss.[37] Despite the hassles that changing workplaces can entail, it can feel like a simpler prospect than to work through differences with a difficult person, especially one who's higher up the ladder.

This move away by changing jobs usually follows a move away that has happened far earlier: an emotional, mental distancing from colleagues we can't stand. Long before we leave a workplace because of the pressure of difficult relationships, we've usually withdrawn from the relationship in other ways: we've avoided interacting with them as much as possible, delayed on replying to their emails

---

36. Patricia J. Addesso, *The Boss From Outer Space and Other Aliens at Work: A Down-to-Earth Guide for Getting Along with Just About Anyone*, (New York: AMACOM, 2007), 1.
37. Allison Schnidmann, 'New Research Reveals the Real Reason People Switch Jobs (and It Isn't Money or Their Boss)', 5 August 2015 (accessed 19 July 2017), business.linkedin.com/talent-solutions/blog/2015/08/new-research-reveals-the-real-reason-people-switch-jobs-and-it-isnt-money-or-their-boss.

or moved desks. If we're the employer, perhaps we've even tried moving the difficult person to another department!

How do many Australian workers handle the pressure of difficult office relationships? We move away.

Strategy #2: Move towards and attack

Not everyone moves away from a difficult workplace relationship. There's another common response, which is to get defensive, demand our rights and get even. Rather than move away, we move towards those difficult colleagues and fight back.

One online article, 'Five strategies to deal with a horrible co-worker', suggests this approach to handling the pressure of difficult colleagues: 'Don't get mad – get even. Lay future fantasy plans about ways to get even with your colleagues . . . If you bide your time there may come a point when you can inflict massive and substantial damage to the work bully and seriously undermine their career. Revenge like this is unbelievably sweet'.[38] That's right, instead of moving away this advice is to move towards and attack!

How does the world handle the pressure of difficult office relationships? We either move away or we move towards and attack.

Strategy #3: Love your enemies

But we can take a different approach altogether, an approach that doesn't put our own interests first or opt for the easiest way out. Jesus holds out to us a way of handling the pressure of difficult office relationships that is radically countercultural; it does not move away, nor does it move towards in attack. Rather, it is a way that leans in with love. And it has the potential to be a powerful witness in the workplace.

---

38. '5 Strategies to Deal with a Horrible Co-Worker', 18 June 2015 (accessed 19 July 2017), workitdaily.com/deal-horrible-co-worker. The same article also includes the strategy 'Physically Remove Yourself Whenever Possible'.

In Luke 6:27–28, Jesus explains, 'But I tell you who hear me: Love your enemies, do good to those who hate you, bless those who curse you, pray for those who ill-treat you. If someone strikes you on one cheek, turn to him the other also'.

Okay, so Jesus wasn't standing around the proverbial water cooler when he said these words. Nonetheless, when it comes to difficult workplace relationships, the people who are annoying or oppressing us can begin to feel like the enemy, and these are exactly the words we need to turn to. The idea of leaning in and loving your enemies and turning the other cheek towards those who have already struck you – some suggest that these are the most revolutionary words that Jesus ever spoke. But what do they actually mean?

Many Bible commentators agree that the idea of being struck on the cheek is more about *insult* than *assault*.[39] In Jesus' day, to slap the cheek was a common gesture of insult.

I'm hoping that you have never been physically assaulted while in the workplace (although, sadly, this does happen). But many of us know the experience of being insulted while on the job. It could be the snide remark made out of your hearing, which nevertheless gets back to you. Or the colleague who has a nasty word to say about everyone else – so you can only wonder what they must be saying about *you* behind your back. Or even those hurtful words that are said in your hearing when your work is demeaned before others, or a time when due credit is withheld or given to someone else. Many of us have experienced this kind of 'strike to the cheek' in the form of hurtful and cruel words in the workplace.

In the face of such insults, Jesus urges us to respond by turning the other cheek. Let's unpack what that looks like.

---

39. For example, Darrell L. Bock, *Luke 1:1–9:50* Baker Exegetical Commentary on the New Testament, (Ada MI: Baker Academic, 1999), 592, and John G. Mason, *Luke: An Unexpected God*, (Sydney: Aquila, 2012), 89.

A different way: Lean in with love

Jesus is not teaching that we walk away from the person who insults us. Neither does he teach that we should retaliate and insult them back. Both of these actions flow from a posture of self-protection, handling the situation with our own interests primarily in mind. Instead, Jesus gently instructs us to place the interests of others before our own. He tells us to lean in with love – to make ourselves vulnerable by leaning in with our cheek towards the other.

Now, if I present my cheek to a person, there are two potential responses that come to mind. They could slap me. Or they could 'kiss me'.[40] It's a risk. Which one will occur? Jesus says that taking this risk, being vulnerable, is the key to handling the pressure of difficult workplace relationships. We lean in with love to those colleagues who make our life in the workplace miserable, knowing that we might just get hit again. But perhaps we might get 'kissed'. That is, leaning in with love opens the way up for a positive relationship with that person. Instead of assuming the worst of the other person, it leaves a door open with hope, daring to believe that things could be better or play out differently. This could never happen if we always choose only to move away or move towards and attack.

Pastor Timothy Keller puts it like this: 'When Jesus talks about turning the other cheek or not paying back, he means not just refraining from paying back, but hoping for a relationship. You're hoping for that person. You want him some day to kiss you. That's why you turn the other cheek. You don't turn the other cheek in order to get hit. Jesus' whole point about turning the other cheek is to say, "Don't you dare just refrain from vengeance externally. I don't just ask for that. I say to you that when you look at the person who has wronged you, no matter how messed up and how vicious

---

40. Timothy Keller, 'The Inside-Out Kingdom', [sermon transcript], (*Journal of Biblical Counselling*, 19.2, 2001), 42–48.

they've been, you need to treat them with hope, you need to treat them with forgiveness."'[41]

I'm not so sure that Jesus instructed us to turn the other cheek thinking that we wouldn't get struck again, as Keller suggests. No, I think Jesus knew full well that turning the other cheek might just lead to another insult coming our way. However, Keller is spot on in saying that turning the other cheek is the mark of a person who is hoping for a relationship: hoping that someday the person might kiss you, that this difficult workplace relationship might change for the good – something that could never occur if we moved away or moved towards and attacked.

Tend to relationships like plants

Paul Tripp writes that we need to 'live in [our] relationships with a harvest mentality'.[42] Relationships are like plants. They don't just grow on their own without being nurtured.

We can't expect difficult relationships in the workplace to simply improve without any effort. If we only ever plant self-protection, nothing will grow. Rather, those difficult relationships need to be nurtured. And Jesus says we nurture relationships and give them the possibility of growth by leaning in with love.

Each workplace is unique, and nurturing relationships will look different in different contexts. However, a starting point might be thinking hard about the things that we say to those difficult colleagues. 'Every day', Tripp continues, 'you harvest relational plants that have come from the seeds of words and actions that you previously planted'.[43] Relationships, for good or for ill, are shaped by the words that we sow into them. If words have been the weapon used against you by that difficult person in the workplace, then

41. Keller, 'The Inside-Out Kingdom'.
42. Paul Tripp, 'God's Wisdom, Your Relationships', 1 June 2011 (accessed 19 July 2017), desiringgod.org/articles/gods-wisdom-your-relationships.
43. Tripp, 'God's Wisdom, Your Relationships'.

why not respond with words also? But make your 'weapon' words of love.

Perhaps it might mean that, rather than avoiding that difficult colleague when you arrive at work in the morning, you instead make a beeline directly for them. You could lean in with love to start the day, offering a smile and a question about their day ahead. You might get struck with a harsh or critical word – or you might just receive a warm response.

Or maybe your leaning in looks like responding to the one who has failed to give you credit for your work by doing what has been asked of you by them and asking if there is anything more that you can do. Again, this response will open you up to getting struck by them again, lumping more work on you without any suitable acknowledgement of what you have already done. Or it might just surprise them, so much so that they surprise you in turn with a warm response.

HABIT CHANGE

Think of the most difficult colleague that you work with.

1. What do you find difficult about them?

2. What is the most positive aspect of that same colleague?

Perhaps plan a time to tell them this week what you most value about them.

Give, rather than withhold, good things

Often, our response to those that we don't like in the workplace is to withhold good from them. We might withhold knowledge that could assist them in their job, details about an upcoming social event or an opportunity that we know they would love. Conversely, we might give them things, but nothing that they actually would like to receive! We give those we don't like in the office a cold shoulder, a roll of the eyes, a slanderous word out of their earshot or, if we're their boss, an unpleasant task to do. Rarely will we give them something that they might actually appreciate.

But in addition to leaning in with love with our words, in Luke 6, Jesus encourages us to give good things to our enemies. 'But I tell you', Jesus says, 'If someone takes your coat, do not withhold your shirt from them' (Luke 6:29). Rather than withholding good from our enemies we are to be generous towards them, giving them something for their good. Notice how many times Jesus instructs that in this passage: 'Bless those who curse you' (28), 'Do not withhold your shirt' (29), 'Give to everyone who asks you' (30), 'Do good to them' (35). Jesus says we are to lean in with love and give those difficult colleagues some real and tangible good. For example, we might offer to help a difficult colleague with a project that is overwhelming them at the moment. Or we might give that childish employee a positive word about the work that they do. Or we might offer something extra to a client who is always unsatisfied.

Once again, in doing this we leave ourselves potentially vulnerable and exposed – without a coat of our own! As we give them something good, like our time, we will be left with less of it for ourselves. If we give help, credit might be given to our colleague and not to us.

This can take real practice. I know my personal tendency is to withhold good from others, especially if it will mean that I miss out. But we can start small. One man I know used to help himself to a handful of communal chocolates that his boss placed in the work kitchen each week. He'd then head straight to the desk of the colleague that he least liked, smile, and leave the chocolates on their desk. It took him very little effort (and cost very little) but it was the beginning of acting with kindness and doing good towards someone he would ordinarily have tried to avoid. When we begin to practice kindness in small ways, it opens up our imagination to what radical, costly kindness might look like.

I once had a colleague my co-workers used to describe as a 'seagull'. Seagulls do not have a good reputation. They're known for turning up when you're trying to enjoy yourself, steal your food and then leave a mess in their wake. It was an apt description for this colleague, who would take all the help that they could get, with very little gratitude, and often leave a mess for someone else to deal with. It was very tempting to treat this colleague with disdain, and on more than one occasion I joined in with the slander when this person wasn't present.

But what if, with colleagues like these, we were to lean in with love and seek to offer some real, costly, good towards them? For my seagull workmate, I could have offered to help this person with their work when no one else wanted to, even if it meant staying back later at work. On rare occasions I tried to do that for this person, although even then I would still find myself resenting it! But Jesus encourages us to mirror his own character in the workplace: 'If anyone takes what belongs to you [your evening at home] do not demand it back. Do to others as you would have them do to you'.

Pray for those who mistreat you

Jesus gives us one more practical example in this passage from Luke's Gospel, and it is the one I have personally found to be the most helpful when it comes to handling the pressure of difficult workplace relationships. Jesus instructs his followers to 'pray for those who ill-treat you' (Luke 6:28).

I wonder if you have ever tried praying for that colleague who infuriates you? We spend so much time thinking about them, but how much time do we actually spend praying for them? If you have ever made a habit of praying for your difficult colleagues then you'll know what happens – it becomes very difficult to remain infuriated with them! I continue to be surprised (although I know I shouldn't be) by the impact that bringing a person before God in prayer has on my feelings towards the person I dislike. I can't help but feel more positively towards them as I take the time to do something as extraordinary as praying for them.

And prayer does more than simply change the way I feel towards a person. As God answers our prayers for them and our relationship with them, the relationship itself often begins to change.

HABIT CHANGE

1. Who is like a seagull in your workplace? What reasons do you often think of for not helping them?
2. What is one practical thing that you can do for them this week, even if it may come at some cost to you?
3. Before reading any further, take a moment to also pray for that person. If you have a prayer diary, consider adding them to your weekly prayer list.

Be a radical witness

All of this acting with love towards our colleagues might on the one hand sound fairly ordinary. In most workplaces I have been in I have seen wonderful acts of love between colleagues, none of whom are followers of Jesus. But that's not the kind of love that Jesus is calling his followers to in this passage. 'If you love those who love you, what credit is that to you? Even sinners love those who love them. And if you do good to those who are good to you, what credit is that to you? Even sinners do that. And if you lend to those from whom you expect repayment, what credit is that to you? Even sinners lend to sinners, expecting to be repaid in full' (Luke 6:32–34).

Rather, the call of this passage is to pray for your *enemies*, to do genuine good towards those who *harm* you, to turn the other cheek towards those who *insult* you. It's the call to love your enemies. As one writer puts it, 'To return evil for evil is normal, it is human. To return good for good is normal, it is human. To return evil for good is devilish. But to return good in the face of evil – this is the way of godliness'.[44]

It is also a profound witness. Author Eric Metaxas writes, 'Love for enemies is the real difference between dead religion and a living faith in the God of the Scriptures'.[45] Love for enemies is the difference between religious types who, when they find a beaten and bloody traveller on the side of the road who is a longstanding enemy of theirs, literally move away, crossing to the other side of the street, and a good Samaritan who doesn't move away but leans in with love (Luke 10:30–35).

To love those colleagues that you find difficult in the workplace, those that you might even call your enemies, will not go unnoticed.

---

44. David Cook, *The Unheeded Christ: Jesus Demands Serious Obedience*, (Tain, UK: Christian Focus, 2008), 20.
45. Eric Metaxas, *No Pressure, Mr. President: The Power of True Belief in a Time of Crisis*, (Nashville: Nelson Books, 2013), 51.

And in not going unnoticed, it becomes a powerful testimony to the one who has loved us most extravagantly like this. For how does the God of the universe respond towards us, his infuriating, difficult, wayward creatures? Does he move away and ignore us? Does he respond with anger and attack us? Or does he lean in, literally enter in to his very creation, and love? This is precisely what he does. When he is physically struck, he turns the other cheek and is struck again. At the cross he is stripped, not just of his coat but completely naked. And on the cross, does he condemn his enemies? No, he prays for them, 'Father, forgive them for they know not what they do' (Luke 22:34). He gives the most extravagant gift for his enemies, his very life, so that we might receive from him some real good – the greatest good, which is life in him.

'But love your enemies, do good to them . . . and you will be children of the Most High because he is kind to the ungrateful and wicked. Be merciful, just as your Father is merciful' (Luke 6:35–36). As you handle the pressure of difficult colleagues by leaning in with love, you give both them, and your colleagues watching on, a glimpse of what God has been like to you.

Here lies the power to love: when we remember how God has treated us, his enemies, we are empowered to go and love our enemies in the same way. As we are melted afresh by his extraordinary love towards us, we cannot help but 'go and do likewise' (Luke 10:37). Empowered by his Spirit, the Spirit of the one who loves so generously, we are enabled to begin to love like this also.

HEART CHANGE

Simply trying really hard in our own strength to love our difficult colleagues will never work long term. It is only empowered by the Spirit, and through the example of Jesus' love for us, that we can ever 'go and do like-wise'. That is, our heart is moved to love like this.

Some practical ways we might seek to have our heart moved are:

1. Memorise Romans 5:6–8.
2. Pray for the Holy Spirit to give you a heart like Jesus.
3. Ask a Christian friend to share with you their personal testimony. Sometimes hearing about the extravagant love that God has shown to others can remind us afresh of the great love he has shown to us.

But what about . . .

However a question that often comes at this point, and rightly so, is: 'When is it right to challenge injustice in the workplace?' When might turning the other cheek actually enable harm to continue in an organisation? And is it ever right to leave, to move away from a workplace, because of the pressure caused by the people that we work with?

These are not simple questions. It would dangerous for me to prescribe a one-size-fits-all solution. We need to consider these questions in the context of our specific situation and with the wisdom and counsel of Christian brothers and sisters. So consider doing just that - don't try and solve these questions alone!

A few things can guide us as we look for answers. First, we do need to take toxic workplace situations seriously. Don't for a minute think that I am condoning workplace bullying by what I have said in this chapter. Workplace bullying is a serious problem, and not something to be treated lightly. Fortunately, many (although certainly not all) workplaces have formal procedures in place for us to report bullying. Jesus' teaching that we turn the other cheek does not exclude us from going down such avenues where they might be available and appropriate.

Second, in some really toxic situations (racial discrimination, sexual misconduct, systemic bullying) where a workplace doesn't take this kind of behaviour seriously or address it with appropriate action, the right course of action may well be to move away and leave. We will consider situations like this more in the following chapter, but for now, know that if you can see no other alternative but to leave a workplace then it's the right course of action. I appreciate that this is not a simple thing to do, especially if there isn't the immediate prospect of more work. So make sure you weigh up a decision like this with Christian brothers and sisters. Let them know the needs that you will likely have if you go ahead with leaving a toxic workplace and can't find more work.

However for the vast majority of us who don't deal with this extreme kind of toxic workplace, but rather just the daily frustrations of annoying people, my hope with this chapter is to help us to resist a worldly approach to handling this workplace pressure. Our world tells us not to be a doormat, not to let other people trample on us, but to do something about it by moving away or moving towards them in retaliation. But let's not be too quick to look for ways out of Jesus' difficult, radical teaching. The temptation with Jesus' instruction will be to soften the cost to ourselves. But in doing so we soften the extraordinary witness that such a life provides. The instruction to love our enemies does not come with the caveat 'but only to a point, and when you start feeling like a doormat then stop'. No, the instruction is clear – loving our enemies will likely cost us and mean that we do at times feel like a doormat!

So when you are on the receiving end of a metaphorical cheek slap in the workplace, let's take time to consider our hearts and what is motivating our quest for justice before we respond. As we rely on Jesus and learn from him, our default responses of self-protection and self-interest will gradually give way to love for neighbour and love for God, helping us to lean in with love.

HABIT CHANGE

Is it your habit to discuss workplace concerns with Christian brothers and sisters? Or do you normally make a decision about work first and then share it with them later?

Resolve to take questions about how to handle difficult colleagues to your Christian brothers and sisters first before trying to address them yourself.

Just like Jesus

If we respond to the pressure of difficult colleagues in the way that Jesus instructs, then we need to be prepared to get hurt. When we turn the other cheek, showing vulnerability in the workplace, some people will inevitably seize on that and use it to their advantage.

But take heart – when you respond like this you're being just like Jesus. 'If you suffer for doing good and you endure it, this is commendable before God. To this you were called, because Christ suffered for you, leaving you an example, that you should follow in his steps. "He committed no sin, and no deceit was found in his mouth." When they hurled their insults at him, he did not retaliate; when he suffered, he made no threats. Instead, he entrusted himself to him who judges justly' (1 Peter 2:20–23).

God is the ultimate judge. All cheek slapping will one day be punished accordingly, if not first repented of and forgiven by Christ. 'Do not take revenge, my dear friends, but leave room for God's wrath, for it is written: "It is mine to avenge; I will repay" says the Lord' (Romans 12:19). He sees and he knows the challenges that we face with those that we work with. But we leave the role of ultimate justice to him. Our role is to follow the example of Jesus, who did not retaliate but chose to lean in with love. Because this is precisely what he has done for us.

HOW TO HANDLE... THE PRESSURE TO CONFORM

Wednesday December 10, 1930, was a fairly ordinary morning by all accounts. A New York merchant walked into the local branch of his bank, asking to withdraw all his stocks. The teller refused, telling the man what a safe investment he had made in this bank. Not happy with the outcome, the man went back to his office and told his colleagues that he thought the bank must be in trouble.

Within a couple of hours, hundreds of people were at the branch on Freeman Street in the Bronx demanding their money. By 8 pm the crowd had swelled to twenty thousand, withdrawing more than two million dollars from the bank. The rumour then began to spread to branches across the nation, and after that day the *Bank of United States* never opened again.

You're perhaps familiar with this story about the bank run, considered to have started the Great Depression in the United States. An aspect of the story you might not have thought about before is the way that it illustrates a very powerful force that is at work in the world: the pressure to conform.[46]

In our modern culture, we don't like to think of ourselves as conformists. One of the great defining features of our era is individualism: I am my own person; I choose my own destiny. We're told to be true to ourselves – to be the authentic *you*. We like to think that we are all forging our own destinies. But how true is this really?

If you dig a little deeper, you'll discover that the mantra 'choose your own destiny' is in fact a great myth. Countless studies have proven that, rather than being the great individuals we might think we are, we have a powerful propensity to conform to those around us. Michael Bond's *The Power of Others: Peer Pressure, Groupthink, and How the People Around Us Shape Everything We Do* is a compelling, at times disturbing, book that documents scientific trial after trial, detailing the extent to which we are shaped by those around us. Everything, from what we wear, to what we believe, to how we feel, is shaped by the community we find ourselves a part of and the people we rub shoulders with.

Even the way we eat can be shaped by others. In one study, recounted in *The Power of Others*, dozens of pairs of women eating together were observed. 'Three thousand, eight hundred and eighty-eight mouthfuls later, [the study] found that not only how much each woman ate depended on how much her companion ate, but that each couple's eating was highly coordinated. In other words, the women were more likely to put fork to mouth simultaneously than separately, particularly at the beginning of the meal'.[47] Of course, some might conclude that the only reason for this coordinated eating was so that the participants could talk with each other. But have you ever sat at a table and taken your cue for when to begin eating from

---

46. Michael Bond recounts this story as an example of the pressure to conform in his book *The Power of Others: Peer Pressure, Groupthink, and How the People Around Us Shape Everything We Do*, (London: Oneworld, 2014), 2.
47. Bond, *The Power of Others*, 5.

others? As *The Power of Others* concludes, 'It feels like we are in the driving seat in our daily lives, making decisions autonomously, experiencing emotions that we ourselves generate, choosing what we believe in (and what we don't). Mostly this is an illusion'.[48]

You don't have to read studies to see that the pressure to conform is all around us. I see it in the way that my kids interact with each other almost everyday: the younger watching the older and, rather than thinking for themselves, simply copying what they see being done. In children it's blatantly obvious. But in adults it's sometimes not that hidden, either!

The pressure to conform in the workplace

Conformity is a dominant force in our world, a very real daily pressure that all of us feel. For Christians, this pressure can take on an added feature, especially in the workplace - a pressure to conform to certain values and standards that don't align with our faith. At times, the pressure to simply go along with the status quo can feel almost inescapable.

During my time as a radio journalist, our industry had the tendency to simply copy what newspapers or other media were reporting without attribution. There wasn't a practice of giving appropriate credit to the journalist who had actually done the hard work to research the original story. My workplace felt that this practice was justifiable because we were understaffed and overworked, so in order to simply keep up with every other media organisation we had no choice but to copy what each other was reporting. It was just how our industry worked: 'This is how it's done around here'.

I think that phrase, 'This is how it's done around here', is usually a good clue that questionable practices are being undertaken. I know that's what it usually means when I use it. Rather than face the truth

48. Bond, *The Power of Others*, 4.

that something might not be right, we brush it away with a comment that suggests all is okay because it's 'how the industry works'. But all is not okay.

I'm not immune to this kind of thinking myself, and it's often taken someone outside of my workplace to make me stop and question the way that things are being done. It's easy to become the proverbial frog in the pot, which doesn't realise it is being cooked until it's too late. It was people outside of my industry who made me stop and ask, 'Is the practice of reporting what everyone else is reporting without proper attribution really okay?'

When I had this particular issue brought to my attention I started to realise it wasn't right. But I must confess I didn't change immediately. Why? Because of the pressure to conform. It's not easy to be the only person in an office who speaks up and says, 'I don't think that this is right'. I imagined the ridicule I would face from my colleagues for speaking up, and so I kept quiet. Occasionally I'd try and change what I was doing, but that only worked if I didn't have someone editing my script later!

You can likely think of examples from your own industry, those practices that are often dismissed with the phrase, 'This is how it's done around here'. And on the occasions when you have stopped and realised it's not right, I suspect you've felt like me. The pressure to conform to workplace cultures is real and can press in hard upon us. To push back or question standard industry practice can result in puzzlement and ridicule – or worse, fierce criticism and ostracism.

The Christian challenge: Be a nonconformist

In contrast to this pressure, the New Testament contains this instruction to Christians: 'Therefore, I urge you, brothers and sisters, in view of God's mercy, to offer your bodies as a living sacrifice, holy and pleasing to God – this is your true and proper worship. *Do not conform to the pattern of this world*, but be transformed by the renewing of your mind. Then you will be able to test and approve what God's will is – his good, pleasing and perfect will' (Romans 12:1–2, emphasis mine).

These verses mark a major turning point in the book of Romans. After eleven chapters outlining 'the mercies of God', the Apostle Paul explains what our response is to be. Put simply, if you have been bought with the blood of Christ then God owns you; your whole life belongs to him. But this is good news! In offering our bodies as a living sacrifice, we give ourselves over completely to living God's 'good, pleasing and perfect' way. It's a great way to live, but a way that will sometimes be at odds with those around us, requiring us to resist the patterns (or culture) of the world. God's good way is frequently a way of nonconformity. Christians are to be nonconformists.

The way of nonconformity has always been a feature of God's people, something that they are called to throughout Scripture. 'You must not be like the nations around you' is a repeated refrain in the Old Testament (for example, Exodus 23:24; Leviticus 18:3, 30; Deuteronomy 18:9). In the New Testament, Jesus picks up this theme in his Sermon on the Mount: 'Do not be like them' (Matthew 6:8). And now the Apostle Paul continues this theme with his words, 'Do not conform'.

The way of the people of God is often the way of nonconformity. It's why the theologian Karl Barth once called Christian ethics 'the great disturbance'.[49] We are people who are called to go against the grain.

Do not conform, but be transformed

So, we are called not to conform to the patterns of the world. But does this mean we are simply to do our own thing, as long as it's not

49. Karl Barth, *The Epistle to the Romans*, (New York: Oxford University Press, 1968), 424.

what everyone else is doing? Not quite. Instead, Paul goes on to say, 'Do not conform to the pattern of this world, but be *transformed* by the renewing of your mind' (Romans 12:2, emphasis mine).

The Greek word that we translate into English as 'transform' only appears in two other places in the entire New Testament, and those two other uses give us a big clue about what Paul is getting at here. The first is in Mark's Gospel (9:2), where Mark describes what happened to Jesus at his transfiguration. There, a complete change came over him: his skin, his face, his clothing shone (9:1–3). He *looked* radically different because his true glory was on display. The other occurrence of this word in the New Testament is not in relation to Jesus, but rather his followers. In 2 Corinthians 3:18 Paul writes, 'And we all, who with unveiled faces contemplate the Lord's glory, are being transformed into his image with ever-increasing glory'.

The point is this. We are not to conform to the patterns, values and ethics of the world. But we are to become like someone else – God's son. The propensity that we have for conformity is to be channelled towards becoming more like Jesus. Jesus himself is the very model of nonconformity. In a culture where you ate meals with people to get ahead, Jesus instead ate and drank with tax collectors and sinners. In a culture that said the religious leaders of the day were to go unchallenged, Jesus instead called out their hypocrisy. And in spite of his incredible power, which should have seen him seated on a throne, instead he got down on his knees and washed feet. So we are to conform to Jesus. And like him in his transfiguration, we too will look radically different to the world around us as God's glory is on display in our lives.

Do not be conformed to this world, this era, but instead be transformed, becoming more and more like the great nonconformist Jesus Christ, and live his 'good, pleasing and perfect' way.

HEART CHANGE

When the Spirit is at work in our lives
we become more like Jesus.

1. What are some ways that you can see that you have become more like him in the last year? Five years? Ten years?

2. If you're not in the habit of keeping a journal, consider starting one. In it, you can document the things you are learning about God and yourself. Looking back on journal entries can be a great way of seeing how God has been conforming you more into the image of his Son.

Under *thlibomenoi*

Yet while Jesus' way of nonconformity might be 'good, pleasing and perfect,' that doesn't mean that it is easy. On the contrary, to live as a nonconformist can be really hard. I don't want to be naïve to the very real pressure that many of us face to conform in the workplace, and the pressure that our colleagues and workplace culture might exert on us. It is a real pressure, and to push back on it can be costly.

In fact, being squashed or pressed is the key way that the New Testament talks about the pressure that Christians might face. The word *thlibomenoi*, sometimes translated as 'pressure' in the New Testament, literally means to be pressed or squashed. However it can also be translated as 'afflicted' and often is used not to talk about workload pressure (or time pressure, or financial pressure for that matter either), but rather pressure that we might face because of our Christian faith being at odds with the world around us.

For example, in 2 Corinthians 4 Paul writes of Christians that, 'We are hard pressed (*thlibomenoi*) on every side, but not crushed; perplexed, but not in despair; persecuted, but not abandoned; struck down, but not destroyed. We always carry around in our body the death of Jesus, so that the life of Jesus may also be revealed in our body' (2 Corinthians 4:8–10). Just prior to these verses Paul has been talking about the identity of Christians as 'jars of clay' (4:7) who are seeking to set forth the gospel to people (4:23). Pressure here comes in the face of sharing our faith.

Similarly, Hebrews 11 speaks of those persecuted because of their faith: they were 'put to death by stoning; they were sawed in two; they were killed by the sword. They went about in sheepskins and goatskins, destitute, persecuted [*thlibomenoi*] and mistreated – the world was not worthy of them' (11:37–38a). Pressure is again connected to persecution because of Christian faith. It's the same in 2 Corinthians 7:5 and 2 Thessalonians 1:7, where the word *thlibomenoi* is used also.

The other pressures that we have considered in previous chapters are real pressures that the gospel helps us handle. But the key pressure that the New Testament is concerned about for believers is this one – the pressure that Christians will face because of witnessing to their faith. In our culture, the pressure to conform to the world around is often felt most keenly in the workplace, where we spend so much of our time and where pushing back can be most costly. It's isolating when you're the only junior employee not supporting the latest cause in the office because it is profoundly at odds with your Christian faith. It's risky when you're the only senior manager in your firm to ask questions about the labour markets your organisation is using because, while they may be legal, you're not so sure they are 'good, pleasing, and perfect'.

We need real help in this pressure, not just to have the boldness to be different, but also the wisdom to know when and how to push back. Nonconformity is not a licence to be a jerk in the office, constantly adversarial, aggressive and stubborn. On the contrary, nonconformity can be profoundly subtle, like taking a spot among the hot-desking crowd when you're actually entitled to the corner office.

How to live in a wheat and weeds world

So how do we handle this pressure to conform? Some well-meaning Christians give the following advice to those facing this situation – just quit your job. If the culture is at odds with your Christian faith, simply go elsewhere. Some people might come up with a list of jobs that they think Christians couldn't possibly do in good conscience, and they tell other Christians to avoid them. Such a solution is not only unrealistic (it's not always easy to find good work elsewhere) but also displays a certain naivety about what living as a member of Jesus' kingdom looks like in this present age. Life is not quite so black and white. So our starting point for handling the pressure to conform needs to be a clear understanding of the age that we live in.

Living in an age of grey

One of the most helpful passages for understanding this is the parable of the wheat and weeds in Matthew 13. This section of Matthew's Gospel contains several 'kingdom of heaven' parables. Many of them help us to understand what the kingdom of heaven will *one day* look like. However, this particular parable reveals something of what his kingdom looks like *now*.

Jesus tells those listening that this world is like a field where both wheat (sons of the kingdom; 13:24, 38) and weeds (sons of the evil one; 13:25, 38) are growing. This world is a field filled with both the righteous and the unrighteous. But then comes a critical detail that helps us understand our present age. When asked whether the weeds should be pulled out of this field, the response is 'No, *let both grow together*' (13:29, 30, emphasis mine). A time will come when the weeds, the unrighteous sons of the evil one, are pulled out of Jesus' kingdom. But that time is not now. Rather, we live in an age when both wheat and weeds grow together, when the righteous and the unrighteous live and work alongside one another.

This has significant implications for how we handle the pressure to conform. Trying to escape it simply by changing jobs and going somewhere that shares our morals, values and ethics often won't work. Rather, we need to accept that we live in an age of grey, and expect to rub up against people of different values in all workplaces.

And just as trees produce certain fruit, so the righteous and the unrighteous will produce righteous and unrighteous fruit respectively. All workplaces will produce both good work that serves and benefits people, and at times work that harms others. For example, I remember once spending an entire morning reporting from a massive factory fire that had shut a major Sydney road. It was good work that helped inform those stuck in their cars. But on another occasion I was sent to report from the scene of a house fire where two young children had died. I remember feeling conflicted as I sought out interviews from grieving neighbours. They were in shock and I was intruding. At the same time, I knew that my reporting could warn those listening and possibly prevent similar tragedies. What I should do wasn't black and white. Living in a grey age, where my work could both help and harm, made it tricky.

So how are we to live in this 'wheat and weeds' world, in this age of grey? Andrew Cameron, in his book *Joined-up Life: A Christian Account of How Ethics Works*, suggests that there are 'four postures' that Christians are to adopt when relating to the world.[50] I have

50. Andrew Cameron, *Joined-Up Life: A Christian Account of How Ethics Works*, (Nottingham: IVP, 2011), 224–229. This next section is in part a summary of these pages in Cameron's book, with my application to the workplace and handling the pressure to conform.

found these postures tremendously helpful in providing a framework for handling the pressure to conform.

Cooperation

The first posture is cooperation. While we live in a wheat and weeds world, we nevertheless can seek to do real good. It's adopting the posture of Romans 12:18: 'If it is possible, so far as it depends on you, live at peace with everyone.'

For example, we might be a teacher who finds ourselves in an education system that at times seems more concerned with profit than the education of children. Nevertheless, we'll seek as best as possible to make the shaping of minds rather than the accrual of money our focus. Or we might work for a law firm that pushes us to increase client numbers at the cost of genuine, personal care. So we will seek as best as possible to take time to be attentive to our clients' personal circumstances, in spite of the pressure to treat them as billing units only.

What this may mean is that, at times, we have to make 'good compromises'.[51] Christian ethicist Oliver O'Donovan explains that there are two types of compromises that we can make. Firstly there are those where we *do* conform to the pattern of this world, and so sin. These are not the kind of compromises I'm suggesting! But then there are examples of good compromise where we pursue a course of action that, while not ideal, nevertheless allows us to do some real good: 'We give up the impossible for what's possible.'[52] Or in other words, we seek to help wheat to flourish and weeds to wilt, at times having to do so within the confines of an organisation that might cause some harm to individuals and communities.

---

51. I am indebted to Tim Adeney and Stuart Heath and their work unpacking Oliver O'Donovan in their book, *Love and Wisdom: Bringing life to the Scriptures*, (Summer Hill: Gospel Groundwork, 2013).
52. Adeney and Heath, *Love and Wisdom*, 90.

For example, the mining industry at times does great harm to the environment and communities. But it also does great good. Who does not benefit almost every moment of every day from some resource (coal, gas, gold) that has been mined? So the Christian in mining, recognising that they're operating within an industry that can harm the environment and communities, will seek to limit that harm and increase the good that this industry does.

A classic example of this approach in the Bible is Joseph in the book of Genesis. He was a wheat man working in a weeds workplace. He accomplished some real good – providing food for those suffering from a famine – but all in the context of working for Pharaoh, a rival to the true and living God. Joseph's work only further established the Pharaoh's rule in the region by making the surrounding nations dependant upon Egypt for food. But it also did real good, saving people from starvation.

HABIT CHANGE

1. What is the good that your work does? Think as broadly as you can about all the potential people and organisations impacted by your workplace.

2. What is the harm that your work does? Again, think as broadly as you can.

3. What might it look like for you to help the good that you thought of in question one to flourish, and the harm that you thought of in question two to be minimised? Think of one practical thing that you can do tomorrow to either help wheat to flourish or weeds to wilt.

Subversion

Sometimes, though, we will need to move beyond cooperation to subversion. This is where we handle the pressure to conform by acting in ways that subvert and challenge the culture of our workplaces. We push back against the pressure we are experiencing, not with our words so much as our actions. Cameron suggests, for example, that Jesus eating meals with sinners is an act of subversion, challenging the culture of his day.[53]

I remember the first time I saw a Christian boss of mine put himself on the worst shift on our roster at work. It was the shift that only the most junior employee ever took. So what was he doing there? Simply, he was subverting the culture of our industry, refusing to conform to what the world said about how bosses should act. Instead he was humbling himself, placing himself below his rightful station, taking on the form of a servant. Rather than conforming, he was being transformed.

A simple way that I have tried to subvert workplace cultures is by saying sorry. If you work in an office where no one ever apologises and then you say 'sorry', that is an act of subversion! You're refusing to conform to the pattern of that office.

HABIT CHANGE

1. What are some examples of the culture of your workplace, the kind of things where people say 'that's just the way it is done around here'?
2. What is a simple way that you might subvert one of those practices?

53. Cameron, *Joined-Up Life*, 226.

Exposure

However there may be times where, in order to handle the pressure to conform, we will be required to do something more than cooperate or subvert. There may come a time when we must stand up to something. 'Have nothing to do with the fruitless deeds of darkness, but rather expose them' (Ephesians 5:11). This is what Cameron calls 'the whistle-blower posture',[54] where we call out harmful practices that our workplace undertakes.

One of the most famous verses in the book of Esther comes when the Jewish queen finds herself placed in a dangerous position before the king. The Jewish people are being threatened with death, and Esther has a chance to speak up before the king, at potential great cost to herself, even her own life (Esther 4:11). She is counselled by her cousin Mordecai, 'Do not think that because you are in the king's house you alone of all the Jews will escape. For if you remain silent at this time, relief and deliverance for the Jews will arise from another place, but you and your father's family will perish. And who knows but that you have come to your royal position *for such a time as this*?' (Esther 4:13–14, emphasis mine). Maybe it is the case that God has placed you in your role for a particular moment where you call out the darkness in your industry, at a potential cost to yourself.

Reflecting on this example in Esther, Timothy Keller writes, 'If you are unwilling to risk your place in the palace for your neighbours, the palace owns you'.[55] It is likely that in the course of all of our careers we will have to confront our own 'Esther moment', where it comes down to a choice between being owned by the palace and being owned by God. Of course, we need to keep perspective; not every point of pressure to conform requires exposure. Some people see Esther moments in their workplace everyday, when in fact they

---

54. Cameron, *Joined-Up Life*, 227.
55. Timothy Keller, *Every Good Endeavour: Connecting Your Work to God's Work*, (London: Hodder & Stoughton, 2014), 123.

are just facing opportunities to cooperate or subvert! Nevertheless, we need to be ready when the time comes to resolve that we will not conform to this pattern of our organisation, even if it costs us.

Separation

The final posture that the New Testament offers is one that we've mentioned already, but have noted that it's one that we shouldn't immediately rush to. In fact, Cameron calls it an 'emergency condition'.[56] This emergency condition is separation; that is, 'come out from them and be separate' (2 Corinthians 6:17). This is the posture we adopt when we realise that our gardening skills cannot handle the onslaught of weeds in our industry. As much as we have tried to help wheat to flourish and weeds to wilt, if our particular industry is so overwhelmed with weeds, sometimes the only option is to get out.

If we are faced with this situation, we are to get out recognising that wherever we go, we will still have to deal with weeds. We live in an age where wheat and weeds 'both grow together'. We won't be naive in thinking that simply changing jobs will remove us from having to deal with weeds. In all workplaces in this age, the pressure to conform will be a constant pressure. Recognising this, and having a framework like the one Cameron offers, will go a long way towards helping us handle the very real pressure to conform.

Finding support from others

There is one other essential resource at our disposal in helping us handle the pressure to conform. In instructing the Romans not to conform, the Apostle Paul begins with these words: 'I urge you, brothers and sisters' (12:1). Paul does not address individuals who are trying to handle the pressure to conform on their own. He addresses a family.

---

56. Cameron, *Joined-Up Life*, 229.

While we need individual knowledge of how to handle the pressure to conform, we also need one another. If it is the case that handling this pressure will at times be costly, then we can draw on the support of our Christian brothers and sisters. As we saw in the last chapter, we don't have to handle the pressures of work on our own. We are part of a community; we can share our burdens with other Christians and invite them to support us prayerfully and in other ways as we seek to navigate them.

Someone I know tells the story of a young man in her Bible study group who worked in an industry where it was virtually impossible to secure clients without over-promising – in other words, deceiving his customers. As a Christian, this was a practice he felt profoundly uncomfortable with, but he did not know any other way to operate. So he shared this concern with the Bible study group, the pressure that he felt to conform. The group counselled this young man to go out and seek to secure clients by making truthful pitches.

It was thought that in doing this there might be two possible outcomes. Either clients would be so impressed with the truthfulness of this person that they, and the wider company and industry, would be won over and adopt more honest dealings. That is, an act of subversion might change the culture. Or it might result in this person losing his job. But the group promised that if he did lose his job, they would be there to support him.

After two years of dealing with clients in this way, sadly nothing had changed. Instead, the young man was made redundant. His act of subversion came at great cost. But true to their word, this Bible study group stood by their fellow member and supported him in his season of unemployment until he found new work. I imagine for this person to pursue such a course of action might have seemed near impossible, except for the promise of the support of his Christian brothers and sisters.

The cost of nonconformity

The pressure to conform is a pressure that all those who are being transformed into the image of Jesus *will* feel. If we're not feeling it at all, that might mean we need to take stock and ask ourselves, 'Why don't I feel this? Is it because I'm *not* conforming to the image of Christ in my workplace?'

As we seek to handle this very real pressure, we need to recognise that at the end of the day to be a nonconformist might be costly. It might cost us a promotion. It might cost us approval in the eyes of our colleagues and industry. It might even cost us our job. But as we resist conforming, we join with Christians throughout the ages who have resolved that 'it is better to suffer than to sin'.[57] It is better to forgo some pleasure in this age and find ourselves among the righteous who 'will shine like the sun in the kingdom of their Father' (Matthew 13:43), which is where the parable of the wheat and the weeds concludes.

What's more, we join with the one whose nonconformity cost him his very life. In view of that extravagant mercy shown to us by Jesus, the greatest nonconformist, we can live joyfully as those who do not conform.

---

57. Karen Jobes, *1 Peter*, Baker Exegetical Commentary on the New Testament, (Ada MI: Baker Academic, 2005), 4.

5

HOW TO HANDLE... THE PRESSURE TO STAY ON TOP OF EVERYTHING

Thomas Edison is best known as the man who invented the light bulb. Perhaps less well know is the reason *why*. Born in the United States in the late 1800s Edison was, according to some accounts, a workaholic. He would often be at his desk late into the night, even into the early hours of the morning. According to some reports, on the night that his first wife died he had to be called home from his office at 2 am so that he could at least be there when she took her final breath. However, he was soon back at work.[58]

Edison loved his work, but there was an obstacle to him accomplishing all that he wanted to do. Something that stopped him each day from working, and that was the night. As one writer puts it, 'For Edison there were never enough hours in the day for work. So he

58. Michael McGirr tells this story of Edison in *The Lost Art of Sleep*, (Sydney: Piccador, 2009), 7–9.

made more'.[59] Behind the invention of the light bulb, so the story goes, was a man determined to never stop working.

On the night of October 22, 1879, Edison got a bulb to burn for over twelve hours. Within days he had one that burned for 100 hours. 'It would not be long before eating by candlelight became something special . . . Edison would move heaven, earth and New York City to create a commercial network for electric light. Now the whole world could stay up late . . . Edison had murdered sleep. He was part of a gang of assassins who've been at work since light divided night from day'.[60]

Edison provided a 'solution' to a problem many of us often face: not having enough hours in the day to keep on top of everything. With the invention of the light bulb, Edison gave us the false idea that we no longer have to stop when the sun goes down, that we actually have the time to keep everything in our lives under control. And so we stay up later and later, working.

In spite of the extra hours, the problem of time remains. Recently when I was feeling particularly swamped with work, I expressed to a friend that not only are there not enough hours in the day, sometimes it's as if there aren't enough days in the week! There is just never enough time to keep on top of all the responsibilities that I have.

Divorcing sleep from night and day

The enormous impact of Edison's work – blending night with day – can hardly be overstated. But as well as giving us more hours in the day to try and keep everything in our lives under control, his invention also disrupted a beautiful harmony between the way the world works and the way our bodies work.

---

59. McGirr, *The Lost Art of Sleep*, 13.
60. McGirr, *The Lost Art of Sleep*, 13.

Our bodies work to something called circadian rhythms, a 24-hour inbuilt pattern that tells our bodies when to sleep, wake up and eat. Connected to these rhythms is a hormone called melatonin. According to the Australia Sleep Health Foundation, melatonin levels are controlled by this inbuilt body clock. The amount of melatonin that our body produces can be impacted by light: it *decreases* when we are in bright light, but *increases* at night when it begins to get dark. The point of all this is that melatonin 'helps establish the conditions [in our body] for sleep'.[61] That is, when melatonin levels rise, this tells our body, 'It's time for bed!'

Which is why Edison's invention of the light bulb is just so significant. Previously, when the sun set and the day began to get darker, our bodies would begin to produce more melatonin, communicating to us that it was soon time for bed. But if you can have light on late into the night . . . well, you begin to see the problem! The beautiful rhythm between the day and night and our bodies was broken with the invention of the light bulb.

More recent technological developments have only exacerbated the problem. Do you know the number one culprit impacting our sleep today? The mobile phone. Devices like mobiles emit a type of light known as blue light. 'While light of any kind can suppress the secretion of melatonin, blue light at night does so more powerfully'.[62] In other words, looking at your phone tells your body to stop producing melatonin, interfering with your body's ability to prepare for sleep.

As evidence of this, a group of Harvard researchers tested the effects of six and a half hours of blue light compared to another

61. 'Melatonin', Sleep Health Foundation, 8 October 2011 (accessed 19 July 2017) sleephealthfoundation.org.au/pdfs/melatonin.pdf.
62. 'Blue Light Has a Dark Side', Harvard Health Publications, 2 September 2015 (accessed 19 July 2017), health.harvard.edu/staying-healthy/blue-light-has-a-dark-side.

form of light known as green light. 'The blue light suppressed melatonin for about twice as long as the green light and shifted circadian rhythms by twice as much'.[63] Basically, the light from your mobile is really bad in helping you prepare to sleep. So why do I usually spend time looking at my mobile phone right about the time I'm meant to be sleeping? You guessed it! I check emails in a bid to try and stay in control and on top of everything!

So, both light bulbs and mobile phones impact our sleep, not just because they facilitate us staying up later, but also because they impact the rhythms of our body.

Awake with worry

But it's not just our light bulbs and phones that can cause our sleep problems. It's also the content on the phone that can set our minds racing as we are trying to wind down for the day. I've lost count of the number of times that I've lain in bed at night preparing to go to sleep, only to have 'one last check' of my phone and discover an email about a work problem or a family problem. Suddenly I'm wide awake, my mind buzzing.

Then there's the waking in the night with concern and worry about life's problems. Whether it's work, family, health or finances, many of us know the experience of being wide awake at 3 am, filled with worry about how to solve the troubles in our lives. Brigid Schulte confesses to this in her book *Overwhelmed: Work, Love and Play When No One Has the Time*. 'At night I often wake in a panic about all the things I need to do or didn't get done. I worry that I'll face my death and realise that my life got lost in this frantic flotsam of daily stuff'.[64] Brigid is not alone. I too have known the 3 am hour

63. 'Blue Light Has a Dark Side'.
64. Schulte, *Overwhelmed*, 5.

far too well, lying awake with concern and worry about the pressures of life, which always seem far more overwhelming in the still, dark hours of the night.

Perhaps part of the reason for our sleep problem is the nature of work today that we considered in chapter two. Huda Akil, a neuroscientist at the University of Michigan, explains:

> As a farmer if there was a freeze that destroyed your crops, that might've stressed you, but it wasn't your fault. As a knowledge worker you're expected to be in charge of everything. And when things go wrong, it is your fault. The thinking is, you could have planned more, or you should have anticipated what went wrong. That combination of having a lot coming at you and of shifting away from physical work – which does help cope with stress – and not even being able to say, 'It's not my fault, I surrender to higher forces' whether you believe it's weather or God – that's been taken away.[65]

In knowledge work, there's an added pressure to keep on top of everything. And that's a heavy burden for us to carry, a burden that can keep us up late at night trying to stay in control, or waking at night with worry that we can't manage it all.

The size of the problem

The sheer size of the sleep problem in countries like Australia is extraordinary when you stop and consider the numbers. According to the Australasian Sleep Association, one third of us suffer from sleep problems, while 35% of us say we don't feel refreshed when we

---

65. Quoted in Schulte, *Overwhelmed*, 62–63.

wake up.[66] A similar number report waking frequently during the night. One article, 'Restless Nights and Zombie Days: Sleep Anxiety is the New Zeitgeist', reported that one in five Australians get less than six hours of sleep a night.[67] According to a 2016 Sleep Health Survey of Australian adults, a quarter of us (26%) use the internet most or every night of the week just before bed, while nearly a quarter (23%) say their typical weekday routine of work and home duties doesn't allow them to get enough sleep.[68]

And it's having an impact on our work and economy. A 2011 Deloitte Access Economics report found that the total cost associated with sleep disorders in Australia was $36.4 billion.[69] A concerning 29% of adults also report making errors at work because of tiredness, while 17% have missed work because they were tired.[70] Type 'Why am' into Google and, before you can type the next word, Google's auto function will predict your search terms to be 'Why am I always tired'! We are a tired population. And if this is not you, then it is someone in your family, or your neighbour, or the person sitting next to you at work. The pressure to keep on top of everything and in control is impacting our sleep.

---

66. Kim Arlington, 'Why Australians Aren't Getting Enough Sleep', 4 January 2017 (accessed 19 July 2017), smh.com.au/lifestyle/health-and-wellbeing/waking-up-is-hard-to-do-why-australians-arent-getting-enough-sleep-20161201-gt1k9y.html.
67. Julie Power, 'Restless Nights and Zombie Days: Sleep Anxiety is the New Zeitgeist', 10 June 2016 (accessed 19 July 2017), smh.com.au/national/restless-nights-and-zombie-days-sleep-anxiety-is-the-new-zeitgeist-20160610-gpg9nb.html.
68. Robert Adams et al, *Report to the Sleep Health Foundation 2016 Sleep Health Survey of Australian Adults*, (accessed July 19 2017), sleephealthfoundation.org.au/pdfs/surveys/SleepHealthFoundation-Survey.pdf.
69. 'Re-awakening Australia: The Economic Cost of Sleep Disorders in Australia', (accessed 19 July 2017), deloitte.com/au/en/pages/economics/articles/sleep-health.html.
70. Adams et al, *Report to the Sleep Health Foundation.*

The problem of 'presenteeism'

It's not just our sleep that is being compromised. The pressure to keep on top of everything also lies behind the huge numbers of us who admit to not taking time off work when we are sick. On a recent occasion, when I actually conceded that I couldn't keep going and needed a sick day, I (coincidentally?) stumbled across an article in my Twitter feed that reported 'sick workers who turn up at the office are costing the Australian economy $34 billion dollars a year through lost productivity'. The report stated that 'presenteeism costs businesses money through lost productivity, and because sick staff end up infecting their colleagues. Presenteeism – employees attending work when they are unwell or in some way incapacitated – costs employers significantly more than absenteeism'.[71] According to other research, 34% of Australians say that they did not take any days off work in the past twelve months due to sickness.[72]

Neither of these reports explored the reasons behind this presenteeism. However, I know why I don't like taking a sick day. It's the same reason I stay up late working, or wake with worry during the night – I'm trying to keep on top of everything and in control.

Paying us to sleep

To try and solve these problems, all sorts of solutions are being offered, including employers paying their staff to sleep! To help counter lack of productivity due to sleep debt, Mark Bertolini, CEO of Aetna, a US health insurance company, offered his employees

---

71. John Carney, 'Sick Workers Costing Australian Economy 34 Billion a Year', 12 June 2016, accessed 19 July 2017, dailymail.co.uk/news/article-3535112/Sick-workers-costing-Australian-economy-34-billion-year-says-Centre-International-Economics-report.html.
72. afuturethatworks.org.au/reports, accessed 19 July 2017.

Fitbit® fitness trackers to monitor how much sleep they were getting. Those who slept seven hours each day (including naps) for twenty nights in a row got paid a US $25-a-day bonus. And apparently it worked; the company reported an increase in employee productivity by sixty-nine minutes extra each month since implementing the sleep pay bonus.[73] However, for some workers, letting your boss know how much and when you sleep might be a step too far!

In some Australian schools you can now take 'sleep hygiene lessons' where children are taught bedtime routines as part of life-skills programs.[74] And books about sleep are flooding the market, one of the most popular being *The Sleep Revolution: Transforming Your Life, One Night at a Time* by Huffington Post founder Arianna Huffington. We're desperate for solutions to our sleep troubles.

Sleep: God's solution to our control issues

However while many of these methods may help to some degree, all of them fail to get to the heart of the problem. That's because there's an underlying problem. Look deeper than the sleep problems, and for many of us you'll find a heart problem. It's a heart problem that the Bible, and the psalms in particular, diagnoses as the persistent inclination to believe that we can, and should, be in control, rather than resting in the sovereign God who controls all things. And our sleep patterns in particular can expose this belief.

Psalms 4 and 127 are two psalms that reveal this connection between sleep and God's sovereignty. Psalm 4 begins with the psalmist in some kind of distress. 'Answer me when I call to you,

---

73. Matthew J. Belvedere, 'Why Aetnas CEO Pays Workers up to $500 to Sleep', 5 April 2016 (accessed 19 July 2017), cnbc.com/2016/04/05/why-aetnas-ceo-pays-workers-up-to-500-to-sleep.html.
74. Madonna King, *Being 14*, (Sydney: Hachette, 2017), 59.

my righteous God. Give me relief from my distress; have mercy on me and hear my prayer' (4:1). And yet it closes with these words: 'In peace I will lie down and sleep' (4:8). Throughout the psalm we hear possible reasons for his distress, but also, significantly, two reasons for his ability to sleep well, despite his circumstances.

Most Bible commentators suggest three possible reasons for his distress. It might be because his reputation is being slandered (4:2), or it might be related to financial concerns (4:7), or it might be because he worships the true and living God but is surrounded by many who don't (4:2, 5). Or it might be a combination of all three! Whatever the exact reason is, the psalmist describes a situation that could easily keep us up late trying to solve things or cause us to awake with worry. And this is what makes the final verse of this psalm so extraordinary. In spite of his distress, the psalmist sleeps in peace. It's important to note that the psalmist's situation has not improved during the course of this psalm. No, this is peaceful sleep *in the midst* of distress.

Verses 7 and 8 explain how. Firstly, the psalmist is able to sleep well because God is his all-satisfying treasure. 'You have filled my heart with joy, when their grain and new wine abound' (4:7). There is a comparison going on in this verse. Rather than wanting more of what those around him have got – abundant grain and new wine – the psalmist rejoices in what he's already got plenty of – God! His heart finds joy not in his reputation, finances, work achievements, health and so on, but in God: '*you* have filled my heart with joy'. This is something we explored in chapter one, but here we see another implication of resting in the all-satisfying God – it can help our sleep! Because the psalmist is filled up with joy in God, he doesn't need to stay up late chasing other 'things', or lie awake with worry, concerned about how to accumulate or protect those things. Instead he can lie down and sleep in peace.

HEART CHANGE

1 What sorts of things keep you up late at night? What sorts of things do you wake up and worry about during the night?

2 To what extent do you think your sleeplessness might be caused by an overvaluing of these (oftentimes good) things?

3 Consider memorising the verses we looked at in chapter one: Psalm 73:25–26. Remind yourself that even when the things that keep you awake are good things, they cannot replace the all-satisfying God.

The one who is in control

But there is another reason why the psalmist is able to sleep well, and it is the biggest reason of all. The psalmist's secret to a good night's sleep is that God is ultimately in control of all things. Not him. Not you. And not me.

'In peace I will lie down and sleep, for *you alone*, Lord, make me dwell in safety' (4:8, emphasis mine). The psalmist is able to sleep in peace in the midst of distress because he rests in the hands of 'you alone', the only one who is able to ultimately protect him and keep him safe. This is the voice of someone who has entrusted their whole life into the hands of a sovereign God. You alone protect, watch over, guard and keep me safe, God. You alone are the one in control of all things. Not me.

'Rising early and staying up late'

If Psalm 4 gives us the positive example, Psalm 127 shows us how things can go wrong. It's a psalm about work. Verse one speaks about our daily building, labouring and toiling, and then our watching and protecting of the work that we have done – all good things to spend our days doing.

But alongside all this good building and protecting, another word appears. Three times in just two verses, the psalmist uses the word 'vain', a word that speaks of transience, of that which is fleeting and passing. The psalmist says that our building, our watching and our toiling is done in vain (it will be transient and fleeting) 'unless the LORD builds . . . unless the LORD watches' (127:1). This psalm is not anti-work; rather it warns that if all our work is undertaken apart from God then it is done in vain. If we labour in our own strength, thinking that we are ultimately in control and that the outcome rests entirely in our hands, then the psalmist says this is vanity.

And not only is it vanity, but it will impact our sleep. 'In vain you rise early and stay up late, toiling for food to eat – but he grants sleep to those he loves' (127:2). The first half of this verse can be translated as 'eating the bread of anxious toil'. When the outcome rests entirely on you, it is a heavy burden to carry, which inevitably only leads to anxious sleeplessness.

'But he grants sleep to those he loves'. For the one loved by God, resting in his ultimate sovereign control over all things, God grants this person sleep. They can sleep and leave the running of the world up to him. Peaceful, restful sleep is for the one who acknowledges that self-sufficiency is an illusion. The notion that we must be in control and keep on top of everything ourselves is a complete fiction.

I'll be honest. Forgetting this truth is the number one reason why my sleep gets disturbed – either staying up late or rising early to try to keep on top of everything, and waking with worry in between. Thinking that I'm ultimately the one in control of everything in my life and trying to find ways to solve all of my problems has caused me to lose plenty of sleep.

But I know I'm not alone in this. We live in a culture that tells us that sleep is for the weak: 'if you snooze, you lose'. Our workplaces place a premium on planning for every potential outcome, mitigating against surprises, orchestrating circumstances so that things work out how we hope. Showing signs of weakness, or admitting an inability to control everything, are unacceptable and must be hidden at all costs. The one who never sleeps is commended.

I remember watching a press conference held by then US President Barack Obama, in which he announced the appointment of John Brennan as the new head of the CIA. Prior to that role, Brennan had experience in counterterrorism and national security. In making the case for Brennan being the man for the job, Obama listed this as being one of Brennan's strengths: 'I don't know anyone who works harder than him. He once told me, "I don't do down time'. I'm not sure he's slept in four years."' Brennan's ability to work hard and go without sleep was considered a badge of honour.

And yet, the psalms tell us an entirely different story. For a while we might be able to keep up the illusion that we can manage everything, or stay in control and on top of everything. The reality is, we can't. Far from being considered a badge of honour, the Bible considers the quest for control a vain pursuit that leads to anxiety.

The beautiful, inefficient design of sleep

And this is precisely why God has made us to sleep. If you ask a neurophysiologist why we need to sleep, they will tell you that sleep is when neurochemicals are replenished. If you ask a psychiatrist, they will tell you that sleep is when our memory is consolidated. If you ask a physician, they will tell you that sleep has a metabolic function. All of this is undoubtedly true.

When you think about it, though, sleep is incredibly inefficient. For one third of our lives we are doing absolutely nothing! Imagine that you created a product but it only worked for two-thirds of the time. Any employer would send you back to the drawing board and tell you not to return until you'd made something that worked one hundred per cent of the time. So what was God thinking in making his creatures completely inefficient for one third of the time?

Simply, that sleep would be a daily reminder that we're not ultimately in control – that we can't do everything or look after everything. On the contrary, only God is in control of all things and can keep on top of everything, which is why he neither 'slumbers nor sleeps' (Psalm 121:4).

American author John Piper puts it like this: 'Once a day God sends us to bed like patients with a sickness. The sickness is a chronic tendency to think we are in control and that our work is indispensable. To cure us of this disease God turns us into helpless sacks of sand once a day. How humiliating to the self-made corporate executive that he has to give up all control and become as limp as a suckling infant every day. Sleep is a daily parable that God is God and we are mere humans'.[75] The fact that we have this reminder built into every single day of our lives suggests that God knew we would be prone to forget it!

When we come to the New Testament, we find the very same truths being taught by Jesus. In Matthew 6 he commands us not to worry, even about essentials like food and clothing. Why? Because 'your heavenly Father knows that you need them' (6:32), and if he provides them for the birds in the air and the flowers in the field, then of course he will look after you too.

So don't worry. Don't toil anxiously. Don't stay up late trying to keep on top of everything or lie awake with worry. Because you're not in control of all things and can't keep on top of everything. But you trust in a God who is. So, in spite of whatever distress we might be facing, we can lie down and sleep in peace. 'When can we have

75. John Piper, 'A Brief Theology of Sleep', 3 August 1982 (accessed 19 July 2017), desiringgod.org/articles/a-brief-theology-of-sleep.

any deeper sense of God's power and working than in the hour when our hands lay down their work and we commit ourselves to the hands of God?'[76]

HEART CHANGE

1. In what ways do you forget that God is sovereignly in control of all things?

2. What is causing you the most worry in your life at the moment? Why not commit it to the sovereign God in prayer right now.

How to get more sleep

It's easy enough to say, 'Don't worry and trust in the sovereign God', and yet to struggle with really *feeling* that God is in control. How can we train ourselves to trust in God's sovereignty? While it's true that right belief breeds right action, sometimes, paradoxically, changing our habits first helps to reorient our hearts. Habits flow out of our hearts, but practicing new habits can begin to realign our hearts. This is why I've tried to provide both heart change and habit change suggestions in this book. Sometimes the best way to trust that God is in control is by acting like it! And a key area where we can do that is in relation to sleep. So let me suggest some habits that I, and others, have found helpful when it comes to improving sleep, with the hope that such habits will deepen our trust in the sovereign God.

First, we can minimise screen time at night. I have one friend who turns off his phone one hour before he goes to sleep each night so that he is not tempted to check work emails. He knows that God

76. Dietrich Bonhoeffer, *Life Together*, (London: SCM, 1954), 64.

is the one who is ultimately in control of all things, so he feels free to not be on call every moment of every day. Choosing not to look at our devices immediately before bed also protects us from an unhelpful dose of blue light that tells our body to stay awake. Many of us read in bed on our devices, and so this could be unrealistic for some. Increasingly, phone manufacturers and other companies are developing phone settings or even glasses that can be worn at night to reduce the impact of blue light. So if you can't survive without your device at bedtime, it's worth investigating things like this.

Second, we can create sleep cues. If you've got children you'll know that a night routine helps them wind down and get ready for bed. It turns out that adults are no different. Simple things like dimming the lights in the hour before bed tells our bodies that it's almost time to sleep. For me, I always try to read a fiction book immediately before I sleep. Non-fiction I find causes my mind to keep thinking about things, so if I want to read nonfiction in bed I'll still do that, but then finish with a paragraph or two from a fiction book.

Third, we can watch our beverage intake. Alcohol and caffeine both impact sleep quality, so it's worth taking care with them. For me, I don't have any coffee after 2 pm, and no more than two cups a day. Drinking any more, and any later, interrupts my ability to sleep well. And alcohol, though it can make you feel drowsy and fall asleep more quickly, disturbs REM sleep, so it's important to consider the flow-on effects from that nightcap.[77]

Finally, we can form good exercise patterns. Regular, moderately intense aerobic exercise is helpful in getting a good night's sleep. When engaged in consistently and over the long term, it can improve other health markers (weight, mood, blood pressure) as well as create appropriate levels of physical and mental fatigue. It's

77. Denise Mann, 'Alcohol and a Good Night's Sleep Don't Mix', 22 January 2013 (accessed 19 July 2017), http://www.webmd.com/sleep-disorders/news/20130118/alcohol-sleep#1.

best performed in the morning or early afternoon, however, as exercising immediately prior to bedtime can disturb rather than improve circadian rhythms.[78]

Simple things like these can go a long way towards helping us sleep better. As one writer says, reflecting on Psalm 127:2, 'God may or may not give us sleep – that is his sovereign choice – but if we don't allow time for sleep, he can't possibly give us the restorative slumber we so need'.[79] We need to respect the way that God has wired us to need sleep, and to practice habits that reflect our belief that he is sovereignly in control – then leave the ultimate outcome to him.

HABIT CHANGE

In light of the knowledge that you need to sleep:

3 What are some practical things that you can do to help yourself get a better night's sleep? Implement a bedtime routine? Start turning your phone off one hour before bed? Write down a few ideas.

4 Choose one habit to pay closer attention to over the next few weeks, and take note of whether your sleep improves.

Address your sleeplessness at 3 pm, not 3 am

In addition to these practical suggestions, the knowledge that we are not sovereignly in control of all things and that we need sleep should change the way that we act during the day. I've found that 3 am is not the ideal time to try and address my sleeplessness. Rather,

---

78. Giselle S. Passos et al, 'Effect of Acute Physical Exercise on Patients with Chronic Insomnia', 15 June 2010, accessed July 19 2017, www.ncbi.nlm.nih.gov/pmc/articles/PMC2883039/?tool=pubmed.
79. Ash, *Zeal Without Burnout*, 51.

it's 3 pm, which is the time I'm tempted to say yes to another project or to try and solve another problem, but shouldn't.

Embracing the truth that God is sovereignly in control of all things, and that I can't keep on top of everything – indeed, I'm not expected to keep on top of everything – frees me from the temptation to be a control freak in the workplace. Instead of being marked by a frantic restlessness, I can be characterised by a calm dependence. I'm more able to let things go and hand tasks over to other people, even if they don't do it the same way as me. I won't micromanage, explaining every last detail to those I work with. There is a freedom that comes when it's not ultimately up to us. I'm not suggesting that we abdicate responsibility – rather, that we let God be God and accept our own finitude. It's hard to tell the world about a good God who is sovereignly in control of all things if we're being control freaks in the workplace.[80]

Practical prayer

A final practical suggestion is prayer. And prayer is practical, because it is calling on the God of the universe to be who he says he is: the one who is sovereign over all the situations that we find ourselves in.

I love the words of Martin Luther on this: 'I have so much to do that I shall spend the first three hours in prayer'. I'm not suggesting that we all need to spend three hours in prayer at the start of each day (although you're welcome to do so!). Rather, I love what is reflected in this quote. If we're under pressure, it means we need to be spending *more* time praying, not less. Prayer is often a good measure of how deeply we are depending on the sovereign God. Indeed, prayer may just be the most practical thing we can do to handle all of our pressures. You may have noticed how frequently it has popped up in both the heart and habit change exercises throughout this book.

---

80. Thanks, Shane Rogerson, for helping me see this!

The world will take notice

I know an older Christian man who is now retired. At one stage in his career he was part of a massive retrenchment of staff. In the months leading up to his own retrenchment, his staff team of fifty had been halved to twenty-five, and he knew that the time was coming for him, too. One Monday, he went into work only to receive the news that he was one of seventy being laid off that day. If there is one workplace situation that can cause incredible pressure, and also remind you that you're not ultimately in control, then this is it. And if you're prone to thinking that you're in control, it's the kind of situation that can crush you.

This man can't remember if it was later that day or the next, but he was talking with another work colleague. To this day he doesn't know exactly what he said or did, but as the conversation concluded his colleague looked at him and said, 'You're handling this very differently to others because you're a Christian'. To be retrenched is never pleasant – it certainly wasn't news that this man welcomed. But as a Christian who rested in the sovereign God, trusting that he is Lord and in control of all things, he hadn't let the news crush him. This attitude of trust had not gone unnoticed by his colleague.

As one writer puts it, 'Whenever there are people whose hearts are not fretful or anxious or in a resentful frenzy . . . the world sits up and takes notice'.[81] Regardless of the types of pressure in our lives – whether it is the pressure to have it all, the pressure of ever-present work, the pressure of difficult workplace relationships or the pressure to conform – how we handle that pressure will be noticed. The unpressured soul will stand out in our fretful, anxious, frenzied, busy world where many are under overwhelming

81. John Piper, 'Don't Eat the Bread of Anxious Toil', 28 July 1980 (accessed 19 July 2017), desiringgod.org/messages/dont-eat-the-bread-of-anxious-toil.

pressure. As the gospel changes our hearts and habits, this will be good news, and not just for ourselves, but for those around us who notice and ask why. We can tell them of the all-satisfying God who is sovereignly in control of all things, in whom we rest. And we can sleep.

CONCLUSION: RELEASING THE PRESSURE

Are you feeling less pressured? Maybe not yet! Let's remind ourselves of where we have been and then explore one final way forward.

We've seen how the gospel is good news for us as we face the various pressures associated with work.

We don't need to feel the pressure to have it all because we have an all-satisfying, all-powerful, eternal God who promises us that the best is yet to come. We can miss out now, and it will be okay!

We've been reminded that in Jesus we have a gentle and humble master who doesn't demand of us, but invites us to live a less pressured way.

We've learnt that not all pressure is bad, especially when it bears witness to our colleagues of the rest that we have in Jesus.

We've been challenged to lean in with love when dealing with the pressure of difficult workplace relationships, because that's precisely how God has dealt with us.

We've explored the age of grey that we live in and the different postures we can adopt as we face the pressure to conform in our workplaces.

And finally, we've addressed the pressure that we feel to stay on top of everything, and how we can relinquish our control freak tendencies by getting a better night's sleep.

So what's next? I said in the introduction that I don't see this book as *the* solution to pressure, but as a starting point in our quest to ease the pressure we're under. If you haven't already, why not go back over the heart and habit suggestions and work through those so that you can apply this as specifically to your own situation as possible.

But you might have also noticed a theme throughout this book – the place that Christian brothers and sisters play in our bid to handle the pressure that we are under. God, in his wisdom and kindness, has saved us to be part of a body. So go on and use that body as you try and handle the pressures of work! We can't do this alone. Consider finding a friend to share this book with so that you can then discuss it together. Ask them to pray for you as you wrestle with some (or all) of the pressures in this book.

Maybe you are already feeling a whole lot less pressured. That's great! But again, you're part of a body and if one part is under a lot of pressure it affects the whole body. So why not consider forming a simple book club with others from your church or Bible study group and read through this book together. You could be a great help and support to others who are feeling under the pump.

The ultimate answer to our pressure is resting in the God who sustains us in our pressure, works through it for our good and can relieve us from it. So, last but absolutely not least, commit to daily bringing your pressure to him in prayer.

To close, let me do that for you now:

All-satisfying, all-powerful, eternal God, you know the particular pressures of those who have read this book. You know the burdens they are under and the challenges they face – some that even seem inescapable. I bring them all before you now and ask that you might provide them with the support and care of brothers and sisters in Christ who can walk with them through the pressures of work life. Relieve their particular pressures, I pray. Give them boldness and wisdom to handle them. Remind them of your goodness as their gentle and humble master. And may none of these pressures be wasted, but work great good through them for both their blessing and your glory. Amen.

ACKNOWLEDGEMENTS

I first want to thank Gina Denholm, who not only edited this book but also guided me through the whole process. I have lost count of the number of times that I have remarked to others, 'Gina is incredible at her job'. Her knowledge of the publishing process, attention to detail and wisdom in editing was invaluable. Thank you.

Thank you to Rhe, Ann and the staff at Cherry & Twigs cafe who kept me caffeinated, and gave me a space to spend long stretches of time to work on this.

I also want to thank my colleagues at City Bible Forum Melbourne, Sharon Cheung, David Chan and Stephanie Gear. Your feedback on the manuscript (and the original talks upon which this book is based) was so helpful. Thank you also for shouldering the load of some of my other work, which allowed me to get on with writing.

A very big thank you goes to my boss Robert Martin, whose idea it was that I write this book. Your support, encouragement, and reshaping of my work responsibilities is the reason that it has come to fruition. Thank you for putting the pressure on me (mostly of the good kind!) to make this happen.

Thank you also to all those who have attended Life@Work events over the years and given me feedback (positive and negative!) on my talks. All of it is gladly received, and has hopefully made this a better book than it would have otherwise been. It is you I held in mind as I wrote.

Finally, thank you to my wife Carly. There has been extra pressure on you while I've been busy writing this, but you have handled it with such grace and generosity. This is for you.

ABOUT THE AUTHOR

Andrew Laird is the Director of Life@Work, an initiative of City Bible Forum, and Dean of the Ridley Marketplace Institute. Both roles give him plenty of insight into the daily pressures of work and how the Christian faith helps.

Andrew has a background in radio journalism, holding degrees in media and theology. He lives in Melbourne with his wife and three young children, and likes to fill his weekends with cycling (especially with his kids). He's also the co-author of the study series *In God's Service: Being a Distinctive Disciple in Your Workplace* (Sydney: SMBC, 2015), and is a regular contributor to lifeatwork.org.au

www.ingramcontent.com/pod-product-compliance
Ingram Content Group UK Ltd.
Pitfield, Milton Keynes, MK11 3LW, UK
UKHW020418250726
13967UKWH00007B/2709

9 780648 137962